SOCIAL AND MORAL THEORY IN CASEWORK

The aim of the book is to 'map the logical geography' of an important set of concepts which enter into the theory of social casework – those concerning the individual and society. Concepts examined include the individually orientated values of 'self-direction' and 'acceptance', and those of 'role', 'adjustment' and 'integration' which express the individual's relation to society. The author's main concern is to see whether a coherent theory of the relationship between individual and society can be given in terms of these concepts and to argue that such a theory is fundamental to casework discussion.

Mr. Plant also discusses what, if any, social or political commitments the activity of casework presupposes, and evaluates the view that casework is 'apolitical'.

LIBRARY OF SOCIAL WORK

GENERAL EDITOR: NOEL TIMMS

Lecturer in Social Science and Administration
London School of Economics

Social and Moral Theory in Casework

by Raymond Plant
Assistant Lecturer in Philosophy
The Victoria University of Manchester

LONDON
ROUTLEDGE & KEGAN PAUL

First published 1970
by Routledge & Kegan Paul Ltd
Broadway House, 68-74 Carter Lane
London, E.C.4
Printed in Great Britain
by Northumberland Press Ltd
Gateshead
© Raymond Plant 1970
ISBN 0 6808 5 (C)
ISBN 0 7100 6809 3 (P)

For Katherine

Contents

CONTENTS

General editor's introduction

The Library of Social Work is designed to meet the needs of students following courses of training for social work. In recent years the number and kinds of training in Britain have increased in an unprecedented way. But there has been no corresponding increase in the supply of textbooks to cover the growing differentiation of subject matter or to respond to the growing spirit of enthusiastic but critical enquiry, to the significant theoretical contributions so far made to its understanding, and to some of the outstanding problems. Each volume will suggest ways in which the student might continue his work by further reading.

This essay on the moral and social presuppositions and implications of casework revolves around the concern of the social worker for 'two welfares'—that of the individual and that of society. It is divided into three main chapters. The first is concerned with our understanding of the central casework concepts of individualization, self direction and acceptance. It is argued that these are all part of the concept of respect for persons, and the question of justifying this concept is considered. It appears, however, that the particular use made of the concepts of responsibility and self direction by social casework theorists also requires justification. Finally, in this chapter, the adequacy of the formulation of ideas in terms of 'the individual' and 'society' is questioned in a consideration of the work of Raymond Williams. In the second chapter the author critically assesses concepts of mental health as part of an attempt to judge 'scientifically' the kind of society that will help people to experience their social life as members of a community. It is concluded that casework involves moral and social commitment, and the final chapter is concerned with discussing the three kinds of commitment that are open—therapy, reform or revolution.

This book is primarily concerned with social casework, but much of its analysis is equally applicable to social groupwork and community work. Other books in this series have a similarly general orientation, but they are focused on developing psychological and sociological understanding of social work and the problems it attempts to solve. The present work contributes to the freshly acknowledged need to develop an adequate philosophy of social work. The philosophy of social work is still taken to refer to a list, as it were, of principles of action or uplifting ideas concerning the justification of social work. Raymond Plant demonstrates the results that can be obtained by applying the activity of philosophizing to some of the crucial terms in social casework. Such activity produces no new list of principles or any self-evident justification for social work, but it makes an essential contribution to the process by which the profession can begin to know itself. Self-knowledge, so often extolled in terms of the individual social worker, has meaning in terms other than the psychological for the profession as a whole. The book links, as the author indicates, with others in the Library and, more important, with the world 'outside' the usually drawn boundaries of social work. As the text suggests, the principles of casework 'appear to be characteristic of morality itself'; they are 'not as it were the private property of the casework profession and subject to professional interpretation and, possibly, change . . .'

NOEL TIMMS

LIBRARY OF SOCIAL WORK

All titles available in two editions, library and paperback

Volumes already published:

Forthcoming titles will include:

Routledge & Kegan Paul

Acknowledgements

My thanks are due in particular to Dr Gordon Rose of the Department of Social Administration in the Victoria University of Manchester who, by inviting me to lecture to third year students in that department in the academic year 1968-9, provided me with both the incentive and opportunity to produce the reflections on casework theory which constitute this monograph. I also have a debt of gratitude to those students who forced me to clarify my too often confused ideas. Noel Timms, the editor of the series, suggested to me many improvements, most of which I have adopted, and for which I am very grateful. I should like to thank Mr M. B. Yeats and Macmillan & Co for permission to quote from 'Among School Children' by W. B. Yeats, and also Faber and Faber, Ltd for permission to quote from T. S. Eliot's 'The Waste Land'.

My greatest debt, however, is to my wife Katherine, who provided encouragement when it was needed and who helped with the preparation of the typescript and with correction. I therefore dedicate this, my first book, to her.

RAYMOND PLANT

1

Introductory and programmatic

> There is a multitude of definitions of social casework.
> All imply a dual concern; to help not only the individual
> in his relations with society, but also society in its
> relations with the individual. . . . The structure of social
> casework exhibits at every point a functional concern
> not only with the welfare of the individual, but also of
> society.
>
> (Pollard, 1962)

This essay on the moral and social presuppositions and
implications of casework revolves around the contrast
pointed in this quotation: between the concern of the
social worker with the welfare of the individual and for
the welfare of society. It will be argued that caseworkers,
because they are involved in this dual concern, need to be
very clear about the relationship between the individual
and society. The discussion and description of this relationship is, however, far from easy, and some of the concepts
involved are highly elusive. This dual concern of the caseworker finds expression in the current tendency to formulate the problems encountered in casework in terms of the
concept of a *social role* which focuses attention upon the
relationship between man and the society in which he
lives. As Dahrendorf points out (1968): 'At the point where
individuals and society intersect stands Homo Sociologicus,
man as the bearer of socially predetermined roles.' The
basic problem to be discussed in this book is whether
casework theorists can offer a satisfactory account of this
relationship in terms of the concepts which they use to
work with the individual, with his own dignity, point of
view, and attitudes on the one hand, and the moral, legal

and cultural claims of society on the other. Such an account is vital to the conceptual coherence of casework, since it is precisely in this area that caseworkers operate. They are professionally concerned with the relationship between the individual and the society in which he lives.

An understanding of this relationship poses problems in moral and social philosophy. The concern of moral philosophy here, is over the relationship which the caseworker deems to hold between the individual's moral standards based upon his own decision and reflection, and those which are present in the structured role morality of the society in which that individual lives. What if the standards do not coincide? What kind of status have the moral principles of the individual compared with those of society? In what sense is there such a thing as social or public morality? Social philosophy is concerned with the relationship between the individual and the social roles which he performs. Is the individual any more than the sum of his social role performances and the social relationships which these performances generate? If so, what is the nature of this self which stands 'behind' the performance? When can an individual justifiably refuse to accept the claims made upon him by society, by the roles which he has to play? Is it possible that some societies may be so distorted that a refusal to come to terms with the role morality of that society may be a sign of maturity and sanity on the part of the individual concerned? Are the practice and concepts of social casework compatible with any form of society, or is casework only possible within a particular kind of society, for example a democracy? All of these are pressing problems for casework theory. Practising caseworkers may not agree but, if so, this could be an indication of a tension between theory and practice, for if the arguments in this work have any validity, these are central problems in casework theory.

The answers given to the questions in the previous paragraph involve certain moral, social and even political commitments, and those who, according to Halmos (1965), come into social casework because they are disillusioned with politics or are merely apolitical are in fact making a mistake about what is involved in the practice of casework. It will be argued that the caseworker, because of his professional concerns, is involved in more political commitments than the average citizen. The precise content of these commitments is problematic. There seem to be several which are open, depending upon the kind of reading of casework theory one adopts. As there is no definitive casework theory, so there are no definitive casework commitments; rather a cluster of alternatives, the adoption of which seems to be a matter for the decision of individual caseworkers. Even though the precise nature of these commitments may be unclear, they are formally of a moral, social and political nature.

At this juncture it may be relevant to say something about this essay as a work of philosophy. Philosophy is, of course, partly a matter of fashion and choice, but contemporary British philosophy is a parasitic subject in that it depends for its existence upon the theorizing of others. It seeks to describe and analyse the concepts which others *use*; it consists in reflection on and analysis of the use and implications of certain concepts within a particular body of theory. Philosophy does not seek to argue for or against the use of particular concepts; it can only point out the problems which may arise within a body of discourse from the use of certain concepts, or from the use of one concept within a nexus of concepts. It can point towards incoherencies, contradictions, shifts of meaning etc., but it is the task of those who actually employ the concepts, who use the body of theory in the conceptualization of their activity, to decide in view of this clearer, more reflective understanding of the relations between concepts, what to do about the problems which are seen to arise. To particularize: a work of philosophy concerned with social casework will consist of an examination of the concepts which are actually used by casework theorists; it will seek to understand the justifications given for the use of these concepts by such theorists, the meaning which these concepts have and the shifts of meaning which may occur between different contexts; the implications which these concepts involve, and the commitments which they represent. This approach accounts for the large amount of quotation in this work; philosophy needs the work of other theorists in order to operate. It has no body of knowledge, no doctrines of its own. In those places where the implications of concepts are not clear, and where the commitments involved are oblique, then the matter is left. Greater clarity could only be achieved by giving the concepts involved a more precise meaning, and it is no part of the philosopher's function to do this. Practitioners have formulated concepts in order to understand what they do and to communicate effectively about it. It would be the height of conceit for the philosopher to propose a new or modified use of a concept within the body of casework theory. In so far as philosophical analysis uncovers problems in the concepts involved in casework theory, these are problems for practitioners only if they feel that the theory does deeply illuminate and indeed govern their approach to practical questions.

This book is divided into three main chapters, the fourth being suggestions for further reading. The first chapter deals with moral and social philosophy, the relationship between the individual and his social roles, and the morality implicit in these roles. The following chapter seeks to understand the relationship between the aims of casework, what has been termed 'the mental health ethic', and the social and political implications of such a view of casework aims. Finally, a chapter is devoted to the analysis of three possible but apparently mutually exclusive models of the political nature of casework. Whether casework should be therapeutic, in that caseworkers should try to help people to come to terms with some aspect of their social functioning, or whether it should seek to change society in the interests of better adjustment and development, and how such a change might be brought about—by reform or revolution. These are models for philosophical analysis; no particular model can be recommended on philosophical grounds.

2

Social and moral theory in casework

> No individual can be completely in tune with the morality of his time.
>
> (Durkheim, 1953)

> Social workers are, in a very real sense, the agents of society who are entrusted with one aspect of the preservation and enforcement of the moral code.
>
> (Miles, 1954)

The central point to be made in this chapter is that caseworkers need, but do not possess, an adequate moral and social theory. A moral theory is required in order to understand and assess the nature and status of certain principles which enter into the practice of casework, and to understand the kinds of justification which can be given to these principles: principles such as 'respect for persons', 'individualization', 'self-direction' and 'acceptance'. A social philosophy is needed in order to become clear about the relationship between the individuals who are approached by caseworkers in terms of these principles, and 'objective' social morality, the impersonal set of norms and standards which are attached to the social roles in which an individual performs, and to which the social worker seeks to help him to come to terms. Caseworkers operate in that conceptual quagmire, the relationship between the individual and society. It may be argued that this way of presenting the problem is not a useful one (Williams, 1965), but it is certainly a dichotomy in terms of which some casework theorists see the subject. Pollard (1962, p. 8) writes:

The tension between the 'one and the many' in social

6

work presents so complex a problem that the profession can hardly, so it seems, develop their study of its two poles simultaneously. On the one hand there is the *individual* who, basically, cannot be helped against his real wish . . . and on the other hand there is *society*, chiefly embodied in the agency, which is part of the reality of the client's situation even in cases where the issues are mainly psychological.

A similar view is implicit in Lurie (Kasius, 1954, p. 33):

As social workers entered into this complex of social and institutional relationships, their responsibilities for and to the community as well as to and for the client became a constant problem for reflection, for definition and action. They began to see that the practice of social work involved relationships to the client—the group served—and to the community with its legal, economic and social processes and institutions. They were soon to learn that this gamut of relationships involved controversial issues and conflicts of loyalties.

Casework theorists do seem to be committed to some kind of dichotomy or duality here, on the one hand the self-directing individual, on the other society. In thinking in these terms, they mirror a traditional way of interpreting and describing our social experience. Williams points this out in a different context (1965, p. 89):

When we examine actual relationships, we start from descriptions we have learned. When we speak of the 'individual' and of 'society', we are using descriptions which embody particular interpretations of the experience to which they refer: interpretations which have gained currency at a particular point in history, yet which have now virtually established themselves in our minds as absolutes.

Descriptions of social experience, which once showed deep insight into a particular mode of social life, have become so embedded into our conceptual framework that even though the context which gave meaning to the concepts may have been lost, we still understand our social experience in these terms. The concepts of 'individual' and 'society' have become a kind of conceptual skin which structures our experience. Williams goes on to make a further point, taken up later in the chapter, which seems particularly relevant to the situation of casework (pp. 89-90):

> By a special effort we may become conscious of 'the individual' and 'society' as no more than descriptions, yet still so much actual experience and behaviour is tied to them that the realization can seem merely academic. There are times however, when there is so high a tension between experience and description that we are forced to examine the descriptions to seek beyond them to new descriptions, not so much as a matter of theory but as literally a problem of behaviour.

The argument of this chapter will be that casework practice exhibits this kind of tension between description and experience, and that a new conceptual framework, or at least a modification of concepts is required. For the moment, however, the component concepts within the assumed dichotomy of 'individual' and 'society' will be examined before possibilities of transcending this dualism are discussed.

The individual in casework theory

In the work of the majority of casework theorists the reader will come upon a cluster of concepts in terms of which the client of the caseworker is conceived, or in terms of which the caseworker's relationship to the client is understood. In both of these cases a certain view of the client emerges. These concepts include: 'individualization', 'respect for persons', 'client self-direction', 'human dignity' and 'acceptance'. The content and meaning given to these concepts by different theorists vary only in the relative importance attached to each concept for casework, and the kinds of justification which can be given for their use. It will be argued that the basic concept here is that of respect for persons, and that the other concepts are merely elucidations of various emphases within that concept.

Individualization

The concept of individualization is defined by Biestek (1961) in the following manner:

> The recognition and understanding of each client's unique qualities, and the differential use of the principles and methods in assisting each towards a better adjustment. Individualization is based upon the right of human beings to be individuals, and to be treated not just as *a* human being, but as *this* human being with his personal differences.

The point is made by Perlman (1957) in similar terms:

> To recognize a person as himself, different in his own way from all others, and to receive him understandingly, transcends simple pleasantness and sympathy. Recognition calls for lending oneself openly to take in the particular uniqueness of this person and of what he is saying about himself and doing with himself.

The concept of individualization is regarded by Pollard (1962) and Robinson (1930) as the foundation value of social casework. It is the absolute presupposition, so it is argued, of modern casework that clients are not regarded as fulfilling certain types and paradigms, but as presenting a particular problem which needs to be considered against its own particular background.

Self-direction

The second concept which is central to the caseworker's account of the individual is that of client self-direction. Indeed Aptekar (1955, pp. 11-12) argues that:

> Self-determination is so important in modern casework philosophy that if one were to pick any single conception without which modern casework simply could not exist, it would undoubtedly be the idea that the client must determine what his own life shall be like and that the worker cannot, and should not try to do this for him.

The point is made in similar terms by Biestek (1961, p. 103):

> The principle of client self-determination is the practical recognition of the right and need of clients to freedom in making their own choices and decisions in the casework process. . . . Throughout a thirty year history the highest possible value has been placed upon the principle of client self-determination in casework: it would be difficult to imagine how its value could be assessed any higher.

Acceptance

The concept of acceptance is more difficult to grasp. It seems to mean something like tolerant understanding; that the caseworker acknowledges the reality of the client's actions however abhorrent they may be to him personally, while at the same time maintaining a sense of the client's dignity and worth irrespective of these actions. The concept of acceptance presupposes that man is not the sum of his actions, that no matter what he does there is some kind of inner citadel of dignity and worth which has to be recognized by the caseworker.

It will be argued that the three concepts, individualization, acceptance, and self-direction are in fact deductions from the concept of respect for persons. They are deductions from this concept in that they are a part of its very meaning. Respect for persons is, on this view, the basic value in casework.

Respect for persons

Moffett writes about respect for persons (1968, p. 27):

> There is a particular value so emphasized by caseworkers, and so involved in caseworkers' thinking that it is impossible to understand casework treatment without reference to it. 'Respect for persons' is more than anything the value which gives casework its particular character.

It is one thing to emphasize the place of this value in casework theory, quite another to give it any precise content. To say that respect for persons is a central value in casework does not mean that all persons are without exception worthy of the kind of respect which a child owes to his parents, or a subject to a monarch. Rather what is in question is not some respect owed to a person because of certain obligations attached to the conventional role structure of a particular society, (that is *as* a farmer, priest, etc.) but respect for a person *as* a human being. Respect for persons seems to enjoin that a man is entitled to respect as a *man* and not in terms of any particular role in which he performs. Again this concept seems to involve the view that a man is not to be identified with the sum of his roles, but rather that he is at least, in part, identifiable as a person who can stand back from his particular role identifications. The philosopher who has written chiefly on this topic is Kant. Kant argued that the moral worth of a man cannot depend upon contingencies; man's moral agency is, in Kant's view, a transcendental characteristic. If it were not, then a man's moral worth would depend upon a quite fortuitous distribution of empirical qualities. A man deserves respect as a potential moral agent in terms of this transcendental characteristic, not because of a particular conjunction of empirical qualities which he might possess. Traits of character might command admiration and other such responses, but *respect* is owed to a man irrespective of what he does, because he is a *man*.

All this is rather vague and metaphysical, and certainly does involve a complex set of presuppositions, probably the most central of which is that a person is, at least in part, someone who transcends what he does, a person who is not analysable without remainder into his role performances. At the moment, however, it can be seen how closely the concept is tied to acceptance, self-direction and individualization. There is no real distinction to be drawn between respect for persons and individualization since the latter entails an attitude to be taken up towards a person which is the same attitude delineated in the principle of respect for persons. Whatever counts as a justification of respect for persons will also count as a justification of individualization. The same is true of acceptance. Part of the meaning of respect for persons is that people deserve respect in terms of their humanity, not in terms of particular actions which they perform. Finally, self-direction, too, is really a part of the meaning of respect for persons. It is a denial of respect to manipulate a person, or to ride roughshod over his principles, conceptions, purposes and intentions. To have purposes and to carry them out, to formulate intentions and to execute them are essential features of human agency, which is a presupposition of respect for persons. If these points are correct, then in order for the caseworker to justify and to use these concepts in theorizing about his relation to his client, it is only necessary to justify the basic principle, that of respect for persons. The kinds of justification which are given to the principle in the literature do, however, seem to be very weak.

Justification of respect for persons

Respect for persons is, in casework literature, more often presupposed than argued for, but what little argument there is seems to fall into three main types: the theistic argument given by Biestek; the possibility of a practical justification; and the view that it is merely a matter of conviction on the part of the caseworker, which can be neither proved nor disproved.

Biestek (1961) argues the case for the acceptance of the principle on religious grounds, an argument which is the theological counterpart to Kant's metaphysical analysis. Man is the child of God, and as such he is endowed by his creator with a certain dignity. This dignity does not derive from his environment, nor is it modified by it, rather it derives from a man's relationship to God. This means that whatever the external circumstances, whatever a person has done, cannot detract from this essential God-given dignity (p. 73):

> This intrinsic value is derived from God, his creator, and is not affected by personal success or failure in things physical, economic, social or anything else. The social failures, just as the socially successful are made in the image of God. . . . Even unacceptable acts, such as the violation of the civil law, or the moral law do not deprive the person of his fundamental God given dignity. In the behaviour which constitutes a violation of the will of God, man is not acting in accordance with his dignity, but does not lose his dignity thereby.

Two points can be made about this justification of the principle. The first and most obvious is that if this is the only available justification, then the caseworker who uses this principle in forming his relationship with his client, but who does not share Biestek's particular theistic presuppositions, is committed to a value supposedly basic to his profession, but for which he can provide no justification. The second point is that the religious justification is at best only a second-order justification. From a bare statement about the facts of man's relationship to God, it might be argued, nothing follows about what sort of attitude ought to be taken up towards men. There is a logical gap between facts and values, because there can be nothing in the conclusion of a valid argument which is not already present in the premises. In this case we are presented with a list of descriptive premises concerning man's relationship to God which are supposed to yield a normative conclusion about the attitude which caseworkers ought to adopt towards their clients. The fallacy of this type of reasoning was pointed out by Hume (1964, p. 469):

> I cannot forbear adding to these reasons an observation which may be found to be of some importance. In every system of morality which I have hitherto met with I have always remarked that the author proceeds for some time in the ordinary ways of reasoning, and establishes the being of a God, or makes observations concerning human affairs; when of a sudden I am surprised to find that instead of the usual copulations of the propositions is and is not, I meet with no proposition which is not connected with an ought or ought not. This change is imperceptible; but is of the last consequence. For as this ought and ought not expresses some new relation and affirmation, it is necessary that it should be observed or explained; and that at the same time some reason should be given for what seems

altogether inconceivable, how this new relation can be a deduction from others which are entirely different.

This is the fallacy which on the face of it Biestek commits. He seems to conjoin a set of factual premises which he takes to entail a moral conclusion. But this kind of argument is illegitimate, as Hume pointed out. As there are only descriptive premises, so there can only be descriptive conclusions. Of course, Biestek could argue against this that a statement about man's relationship to God is not a merely factual statement, because it does have a certain moral element intrinsically attached to it—to say, for example, that a man is the child of God is partly a *moral* assertion, because the role of the child and the role of God as the father involve conceptions of *appropriate* behaviour: the roles involve standards and norms. To say that man is the child of God is not to make a merely factual statement, but rather to make a statement which implicitly refers to, or presupposes, those norms and standards. This point has been made very strongly by Emmet (1966, p. 41):

> The notion of a role, therefore, I suggest provides a link between factual descriptions of the social situation and moral pronouncements about what ought to be done in them. It has so to speak a foot in both camps, that of fact and value; it refers to a relationship with a factual basis, and it has a norm of behaviour built into it. . . .

Emmet also makes a further interesting point relevant to the present discussion—the norms built into role performances are conventional, and this is why it is possible to 'read off' *obligations* from the *facts* of the social situation. To describe a role, for example that of a father, already implies the existence of certain obligations and rights connected with that role. However, at this point the argument goes against Biestek because it is no longer a matter of conventional acceptance that a man has this relationship to God conceived as a father. If we wish to justify and to understand how a particular norm is attached to a social role and its performance, we have to look at the structure of conventions surrounding the particular role. For example; in order to understand the norms related to the role of a father we have to look at the social conventions surrounding this role. We can then, as Emmet says, 'read off' the norms attached to the role. This is not the case in our situation with man's relationship to God. In order to infer what our attitude to a person should be from a statement about that person's role relationship to God, it would be necessary for there to be a shared set of religious conventions. As the role of man here is not generally accepted, an appeal to convention will not enable us to 'read off' the obligations arising from the role.

It is also doubtful whether the use of the concept of a role could help us to understand the obligation of respect for persons. It may be possible as Emmet says to see particular kinds of obligations centred around particular roles. To say X is the father of Y enables us to make some *prima facie* moral deductions, namely that X has a duty to provide Y with food, shelter and protection. But it is doubtful if any role would enable us to infer the moral conclusion that persons are to be respected, since it is part of the meaning of respect for persons that they are not to be respected in terms of empirical qualities such as their *social position*, or their *role functions*. What kind of role could possibly have the norm of respect for persons built into it in the way in which the role of the father encapsulates the norm of protection? Surely the only answer here, would be if one could delineate a specifically *human* role. It could be argued that this is too large an extension of the concept of a role to make it meaningful, although Emmet appears to think the contrary:

> I tried to bring out how the notion of a role has built
> into it a conception of appropriate behaviour in a social
> context in my lecture 'Facts and Obligations'; and
> especially how the natural law view of the value of
> the human being could be read as a way of extend-
> ing the notion of a role to that of a human role in a
> universal moral community.

Biestek seems to be implicitly asserting that being the child
of God is this essential human role, and it is from the
existence of this role that the obligation of respect for
persons arises. However, this still leaves the problem that
this role has lost its conventional status, and is either
totally ignored in the dealings which people have one with
another, or at the very least is subject to a good deal of
controversy.

To summarize this section so far: it could be argued
that the religious justification of the principle of respect
for persons involves a dubious piece of argument, namely
from facts to values; alternatively, it could be argued that
the so-called factual premises concerning the relationship
of man to God involve evaluative overtones, and so the
argument involves deducing an evaluative conclusion from
what are really evaluative premises. The problem then
becomes that of justifying one's adoption of the evaluative premises. Certainly they cannot be presupposed as
reflecting the structure of conventions in terms of which
we talk and think about men in our society.

The second kind of justification of the principle and
a fortiori of the cognate principles of individualization,
self-direction and acceptance, is a pragmatic one. It is based
upon a consideration of what must enter into effective
casework. It is argued that unless the principle of respect
for persons is in fact presupposed, casework will be ineffec-
tive. Biestek makes this point in his discussion of client

self-determination. He argues that this involves the central concept of the dignity of the human person, and that this is essential to the casework process (1961, p. 105):

> Social workers can give abundant testimony from long experience of the futility of casework when plans are superimposed on the client. Social responsibility, emotional adjustment, and personality development are possible only when the person exercises freedom of choice and decision.

Moffett (1968) too, distinguishes the moral aspect of casework principles from the technical. He says of the principle of individualization, which is clearly a part of the concept of respect for persons, that the caseworker considers it is necessary to treat his clients as individuals in order to give them effective casework help; part of the caseworker's effectiveness consists in the fact that the treatment is tailored to the individual's needs. Of the principle of self-direction, Moffett says that it is a reflection of the caseworker's belief in respect for persons, but he goes on to say that the principle has a practical side too, in that it will facilitate the achievement of casework aims; for example, the caseworker is less likely to make elaborate plans for the client only to find that they are not what the client wants at all and that he will not co-operate. Two points could be made about this pragmatic treatment of casework principles. In the first place, it is clear that Biestek does not deal with the principles on purely pragmatic grounds. In the passage quoted above, the principle in question is regarded as effective in the pursuit of certain *aims* (social reponsibility, emotional adjustment, and personality development), which are in themselves moral. Biestek's justification of the principle is pragmatic but only up to a point; the place and function of the so-called practical or technical principle is fixed with reference to further aims which are intractably moral. The second point is to draw attention to Hume's argument in this connection. No statement about what has been found to be effective can entail any statement about what ought to be done. This is not to deny that there may be some merit in separating the technical from the moral, so long as the fact that something has been found to be technically efficacious is not regarded as a justification of what is morally desirable. That certain principles have been found to be useful in casework practice may explain why case-workers now regard these principles as enshrining the basic values of their profession, but this does not, in itself, justify them.

The separation of values from facts, of normative from evaluative discourse, has led to the view that *qua* moral principles, principles such as respect for persons and client self-direction merely express a conviction on the part of the caseworker, a conviction which can be neither proved nor disproved. This is the position which Pollard seems to adopt (1961, p. 11). 'One part of the statement [of the caseworker's concern] usually asserts "the pre-eminent worth and dignity of the individual human being" . . . [this being] a statement of conviction which can be neither proved nor disproved.' A similar position is implicit in Moffett (1968, pp. 25-6).

This kind of view is to be found in a great deal of modern moral philosophy, which tends to stress the rela-tionship of moral utterances to choice, decision, or the expression of emotion. It will, however, be argued that there is no reason for scepticism over the possibility of giving some foundation to the principle of respect for persons, and *a fortiori* to the other cognate principles. Such scepticism is based upon the mistaken belief that respect for persons and the related principles are moral principles of the same type as 'abortion is wrong'. This, it will be argued, is not so. The principle of respect for persons is a *presupposition* of morality if morality is taken as a rational enterprise. Respect for persons is not just a moral principle; on the contrary it is a presupposition of having the concept of a moral principle at all.

Morality and respect for persons

In order to substantiate the assertion that respect for persons is a principle which is definitive of morality, it is necessary to give some indication of the ways in which adherence to a moral principle differs from a merely customary social observance. (For a more extensive discussion of this point see Benn and Peters [1959], from whom the substance of this argument is derived.) There are certain things which may be classified as either immoral or moral, and others which are either proscribed or sanctioned by custom. This distinction between morality and custom seems first to have been drawn by Socrates, in contrast to Antigone in Sophocles' play of the same name. Antigone emphasizes the role of custom in the guidance of conduct when she says of the laws of the community of which she is a member that they constitute: 'Everlasting law, and no man knows at what time it was put forth.' Against this conception of custom with its authority shrouded in tradition and myth, Socrates put forward the idea of critically accepted and rationally justified moral principles. Only those rules which have a point, which can, in Keats's phrase, be 'proved on one's pulses' may be accepted as moral rules and principles. As Benn and Peters say (p. 26): 'This critical rejection or acceptance of custom and law is what is distinctive about morality, just as the critical attitude to theories about nature is what is distinctive about science.'

If we can distinguish between morality and custom in this way and say that customs are accepted on the basis of some external traditional authority, and moral principles are freely assented to after rational discussion, then it seems that we are committed to two criteria, or possibly a two-sided criterion in terms of which we can delineate the moral. These two criteria can be elucidated by reflecting on what we mean by saying that moral principles command assent only after rational justification. Rationality which seems to be an essential feature of morality involves a commitment to impartiality and respect for persons. It involves a commitment to impartiality for a very simple reason. I am not counted as a rational agent if I concur only with the arguments and conclusions of those people towards whom I have a favourable attitude, and disagree with those against whom I am prejudiced. If I say 'Yes, I agree with what you say' because of the colour of your skin, or because of your social class, then I am not counted as a particularly rational being. A person's colour or social class has no relevance to the truth or falsity of what he is saying. To make exceptions for favoured cases, or against prejudiced ones, is to empty the 'rationality' concept of all content. Truth is the aim of rational argument, and truth can only be arrived at by an impartial examination of the evidence, not by the acceptance or rejection of a person's views solely because of his role, colour or class. It is at this point that this central criterion of rationality, the need to be impartial, merges with that of respect for persons. If I am rational then I will respect others as sources of argument, of rationality, and therefore as moral agents. I have to respect a person as a rational agent irrespective of his social role, because the person's role is not necessarily connected with truth or falsity of what he says. This kind of argument leads to the Kantian position, that respect is owed to a person because of his rational and therefore moral capacities; not because of his empirical qualities, his role, his class, his colour, etc. Morality involves the notion of rational assent; this presupposes impartiality, which in turn involves the concept of respect for persons.

Respect for persons is not without justification. It cannot be justified in the same manner as other moral principles; indeed the notion of rational justification depends upon the principle being presupposed. Does this principle involve all that is necessary for the casework principle? It will be argued that it is sufficient. The principle, as understood, implies that a person is to be respected despite his actions, his role, his social class or his colour as a possible source of truth, because none of these features is necessarily related to the truth or falsity of what the person is saying. The principle also involves respecting the interests and claims of others. Impartiality enjoins that like cases should be treated in like manner, and if a man wishes to disregard the claims and interests of others on the grounds of social success or failure, social class or colour, then the onus is upon that person to show that these considerations constitute a relevant and rationally justifiable difference. Impartiality, then, secures the central meaning of the concept of respect for persons relevant for casework theory. So it is with the other characteristic casework concepts. The principle of individualization is implicit in the notion that a person should be listened to in virtue of what he has to say, and not in virtue of his religious, ethnic, or economic type. There are *individual* points of view, and therefore *individual* claims, interests and problems which do not depend upon the individual's social type or position. The principle of acceptance is also implicit in the view that rationality consists in valuing a person's point of view irrespective of his position. Socrates reasoned with a slave in the *Meno*, and the slave's contribution was not invalidated by his lowly social status. Similarly a person must be respected as a being capable of rationality and therefore of moral agency. So too the concept of self-direction is implicit in the understanding of the role of respect for persons argued for in this discussion. If a man is to be respected as a being capable of rationality, then this implies that he should be treated as an end in himself, and not be regarded as an object of social manipulation. The capacity to deliberate and to choose is central to rationality and is the converse of manipulation and coercion.

It has been argued in this part of the chapter that the concept of respect for persons is the basic value in casework, in that the other characteristic casework concepts are in fact part of the meaning of this basic one. It was further argued that respect for persons is not itself a moral principle but is rather a presupposition of morality, and the same is true of the other concepts in that they are deductions from respect for persons. If this is so then it might be asked to what extent these concepts are characteristic of the *casework* process, since they appear to be characteristic of *morality* itself. These concepts are not, as it were, the private property of the casework profession and subject to professional interpretation and possibly change; rather they are the property of any morally engaged person, that is to say, they are common property. If, as will be argued, casework theorists depart from the usual meaning which is given to these concepts in trying to accommodate them to casework practice, then it seems to follow that to the extent to which they do this they cannot be said to adopt a moral attitude towards their clients.

Responsibility

If what has just been argued is correct: that, in particular, respect for persons and self-direction are part of the central structure of social casework, then it could be argued that client *responsibility* must also be a central concept. The concept of respect for persons was justified partly in terms of rationality, which further involves the capacity for deliberation and choice—that is to say it also includes the notion of agency. An agent is someone who *does* something, who *acts* as a result of his deliberation and is not just *acted upon* by the pressure of circumstances. This surely leads to the conclusion that the client must be treated as responsible. A great deal of casework theory and practice, however, seems implicitly to involve a denial of responsibility, and therefore, because of the conceptual connection, of respect for persons and self-direction. Harris (1968, p. 129) draws attention to this:

> It should be obvious that responsibility is an essential attribute of personality. On the one hand our concern for the mentally disturbed is largely lest they be treated too easily as irresponsible when their behaviour may in fact be only socially eccentric and aberrant. On the other hand our treatment of criminals may, with the best of intentions, show insufficient respect if we treat them too readily as patients.

Two examples might serve to elucidate this. Winnicott (Younghusband, 1967, p. 108) argues:

> When a child or an adult *commits an offence* of a certain degree and kind, he brings into action the machinery of the law. The Probation Officer, who is asked to do casework with the client, feels that he ought to apply techniques implying the casework principle of self-determination, but he loses everything if he forgets his relationship to his agency and the court; *symptoms of this kind of illness* are unconsciously designed to bring authority into the picture.

In this quotation a great contrast is to be perceived. What appears to be an *action* of an *agent committing* something is reinterpreted in terms of some kind of *illness*; that is something which *happens* to a person, something which he *did not do* in the full sense of the word, and for which *eo ipso* he cannot be held responsible. In so far as this involves a diminution of responsibility, it also involves a diminution of respect for persons. The same is true of the interpretation of the situation of unmarried mothers given by Bowlby (1952, pp. 93-5):

> It is emotionally disturbed men and women who produce illegitimate children . . . the girl who has an illegitimate baby often comes from an unsatisfactory home background and has developed a neurotic character, the illegitimate baby being in the nature of a symptom of her neurosis.

Here unmarried mothers are implicitly regarded as having diminished responsibility, or being irresponsible. It cannot be asserted by caseworkers that client self-direction and therefore the promotion of responsibility are *aims* of casework (that is to say the client is regarded initially as being the victim of circumstance and non-responsible, the aim of therapy being to rectify this situation), if the caseworker still wants to say that initially he wishes to respect the person. Because of the conceptual connection between these concepts this cannot be done. No sense can be attached to a description of the casework process in terms such as: the caseworker has initial respect for the person, he accepts (in the technical sense) the person, and the aim of therapy is to develop client self-direction and responsibility. These are already built into respect for persons. This is not to deny that many people who come to caseworkers are incapable of self-direction. The objection is not an empirical one, it is an objection against the adequacy of the conceptualization.

Limitations on self-direction

'The client's right to self-determination, however, is

limited by the client's capacity for positive and constructive decision making, by the framework of civil and moral law and by the function of the agency' (Biestek, 1961, p. 103).

In this section a similar but more polemical thesis will be argued in respect of client self-direction. It will be argued that caseworkers, in introducing limitations on the right of clients to self-direction, are in fact abandoning the notion of self-direction which lies at the centre of respect for persons, and therefore are moving away from those principles which are definitive of morality itself. Respect for persons entails self-direction, in that respect for persons is closely related to rationality and hence to deliberation and choice. We only call an action rational if it can be seen to be intelligible according to the standards of intelligibility current in our community, and if it is regarded as the result of choice and deliberation. A purely impulsive action, or a reflex action, does not qualify as *action* in this sense. Self direction, therefore, entails the capacity to choose, to decide and to deliberate. The opposites of these are manipulation, strong influence, constraint and control. Rationality and self-direction imply freedom from constraints, which might be called negative freedom. Another concept of freedom is the opposite of this. It is freedom as positive liberty, that is to say freedom from certain habits or practices in order to promote self-realization. This self-realization is to be attained by acceptance of some pattern of life which is regarded as being necessary for its achievement. Positive freedom is not freedom from influence, but rather freedom conceived as conformity to certain patterns of thought and action. Freedom conceived in this way may sanction influence and interference in a person's life if it is likely to secure the goal of that person's self-realization in the style of life towards which he is being influenced. It will be my argument that

26

casework theory must be allied to negative freedom if it is to do justice to self-direction, but that it constantly vacillates between acceptance of self-direction and positive freedom. The latter element enters casework theory in the manner in which limitations are introduced on the right of the client to be self-directing.

One preliminary point which might be made is that self-direction is a right of personality as such; it is the presupposition of treating a person morally, and this would seem to imply that this right cannot be ascribed to a person by one *particular* body of people. In a sense, however, this is what happens in casework. The following quotation from Hollis (1940, pp. 5-6) brings this out. In the passage quoted the right to self-determination is asserted, but is then regarded as being defeasible by the caseworker:

> Casework seeks to assist families and individuals in developing both the capacity and the opportunity to lead personally satisfying and socially useful lives. This multiple objective is likely to be achieved if the caseworker recognizes that the client must be in control of the guiding of his own life . . . *it is important that the client's right to self-determination exists until it is demonstrated that the exercise of this right would be highly detrimental to himself and to others.*

If self-determination is a *right* of the person as such, then it is difficult to see how its exercise can depend upon the caseworker's assessment of the situation. As was remarked earlier, these principles are not merely *professional* principles involved in casework, they are rather definitive of the concept of morality which we have, and presuppositions of a moral attitude.

Many kinds of clients are regarded as being incapable of exercising the right to self-determination; in particular unmarried mothers and parents of difficult children are classified in this manner. Of the former, Hutchinson (1946) argues:

> In my opinion the majority of these mothers are unable, if not incapable, of making their own independent decision without skilled casework service. It is true that even without guidance she will make a decision but this will be determined by unconscious factors and almost always to the detriment of the baby and defeating to herself.

Lane argues that the parents of difficult children are incapable of making adequate decisions which affect the welfare of their children because of their close emotional involvement. The caseworker, because he is not so involved, will be able to offer advice and influence the decision so that the correct one is made (1952, p. 65):

> The client frequently is not in a position to evaluate his problem by his own closeness to it. We all accept that an essential element of all therapeutic relationships is that the helping person is outside the problem and can therefore see it more clearly.

A similar point, although not directed towards the assessment of the qualities and capacities of any particular group is made by Perlman (1951):

> Where emotional stress or involvement is so great that our perception of what is realistic is dimmed . . . our capacity to be self-determining with judgement and objectivity is obviously impaired. The choices which we make under such conditions are not free choices.

In all these examples there is a similar train of thought. Not all of a client's decisions are to be accepted at their face value by the caseworker, because they are not the kinds of decision which he would have made if he had not been so emotionally involved or if he had a clearer more rational perception of the situation. Noel Timms brings these points together when he says (1964, p. 61):

... client self-determination is concerned with decisions, not whims, and in judging what a client 'really' (or consistently) wants, the caseworker does not rely exclusively on what the client says, but on what is communicated by other means.

The burden of what I have to say here is that this thesis abandons the concepts of respect for persons and self-direction as these were understood in the earlier part of this chapter, and that this important fact needs to be recognized in that it clearly indicates a failure in the conceptualization of the casework process. The conception of self-direction which is allied to the concept of respect for persons involves a negative conception of freedom, freedom as non-interference, as non-manipulation. Respect for persons enjoins that persons should be treated as ends and not means, and that their rationality be respected. Self-direction as modified in the manner indicated above could involve quite a different view. Only certain things which the client chooses to do are to be counted as decisions—in Biestek's view 'constructive decisions' or 'good decisions', in Perlman's view those decisions which are made without emotional involvement at a profound level, and in Timms's view those decisions which are based upon a judgement of what the client really wants. This kind of definition of decision could have unfortunate consequences for the principle of self-direction and *a fortiori* for respect for persons. The caseworker becomes the authority when a question is posed about the ability of the client to be self-directing, and this kind of view could sanction casework influence or even interference in those cases where a client is supposed not to have taken a real decision according to the criteria for decision-making which are given by casework theorists.

I would argue that there is not a definite commitment to this point of view, only a tendency which needs to be taken note of. Noel Timms, in commenting on the argument presented above, argues that it is in fact possible to square the kind of view which he gives with the principle of respect for persons. He argues that we can distinguish between what a person communicates by language, and what he communicates through his behaviour, and that these may in fact conflict. To accept only what is made verbally articulate and to ignore what is articulated in behaviour as a basis for casework treatment is to do an injustice to the *whole* person, and so contravene the principle of respect for persons. I quote from an unpublished note: 'It could be disrespectful (i.e. dismissive) simply to implement one part of a complex whole which a person was struggling to articulate.' Certainly this seems to be true enough, but the literature should take more account of the conceptual complexities of the situation. In order to stress this, the possible relationship between the way in which casework principles are modified, and the theory of positive freedom will be explored.

The first point to be noted is that if only certain decisions are to be recognized by the caseworkers as really being decisions, then it must follow that the caseworker must be in possession of some kind of professional expertise which offers criteria for distinguishing between real and apparent decisions. The second is that decisions which fail to fulfil these criteria are not to be counted as decisions, and in these cases the right of the client to self-direction has to be suspended, so that the caseworker can help the client to come eventually to make a rational choice. The standard of rationality is specified by the caseworker and it implies that the caseworker, in influencing or structuring the decision of a client, is helping that client to achieve the self-direction which he was not capable of exercising at the beginning of the process; that is to say, the caseworker is using his influence to make the client free. The problems which arise for casework at this point mirror similar problems in moral and social theory generally, namely the conflict between negative and positive freedom. Negative freedom is non-interference, the right to make one's own choices, however disastrous they may be, and may be known to be in advance by others who are further from the problem. Positive freedom, in contrast, is rational self direction and realization; the view that man is free only in so far as he exhibits his rationality, and therefore makes rational decisions. If freedom is conceived in the negative manner, then manipulation and strong influence are the enemies of freedom; in the second case, that of positive freedom, they may be the very preconditions of freedom. If a man is in an irrational and emotionally disturbed state, then influence or coercion may secure his freedom. In philosophy the *locus classicus* of the negative conception of liberty is to be found in J. S. Mill (1920), *The Essay on Liberty*; of the positive conception of freedom, E. Rousseau (1947), *The Social Contract*.

Some of the implications of the positive conception of freedom will now be examined. Isaiah Berlin makes a very general point about the impetus to the positive theory of freedom which is very similar to the points made about the limitations on the right to self-direction drawn in the work of the theorists discussed above (1958, p. 17):

Have not men had the experience of liberating themselves from spiritual slavery, or slavery to nature? and do they not in the course of it become aware on the one hand of a self that dominates, and on the other something which is brought to heel? The dominant self is then identified with reason, with my higher nature, with the self which calculates and aims at what will satisfy it in the long run, with my real or ideal or autonomous self or with myself at its best; which is then contrasted with

irrational impulse, uncontrolled desires, my lower nature,
the pursuit of immediate pleasures, my empirical
or heteronomous self, swept away by every gust of
desire and passion, needing to be rigidly disciplined if
it is ever to arise to the full height of its real nature. . . .
What gives such plausibility as it has to this kind of
language is that we recognize that it is possible, and at
times justifiable, to coerce men in the name of some
goal which they would, if they were more enlightened,
pursue, but do not because they are blind ignorant or
corrupt.

If the plausibility of the analogy is questioned let the
reader substitute a word such as 'influence' for 'coerce' in
Berlin's final comment, and then compare it with the work
of the theorists quoted above, and it will be seen that
there is an affinity between the arguments, and at this
point casework theory could be regarded as being committed to at least a weak theory of positive freedom. The
central implication of this view is that someone, namely
the caseworker, knows what the client really wants and
what he would choose if he had the rational grasp and
perception of the situation which the caseworker has. The
problem here is what kind of expertise could possibly yield
this knowledge? Indeed it might be argued that the view is
so paradoxical that no knowledge or expertise could do
justice to its conceptual extravagance. The paradox lies
in that on the one hand someone knows that A is good for
X, while X does not, and this is held to yield the view
that when X is led to do A as a result of coercion, manipulation, influence, or social pressure, then really X
has chosen to do A with his rational self because he would
have chosen A if he had been rational.

The kind of knowledge which might give some kind of
plausibility to the theory might be found in the work of
psychoanalysis. It could be argued that the skills derived
in psychoanalysis would enable an adequately trained

caseworker to distinguish between the overt and the covert, the manifest and the latent, in wanting, desiring and willing. Although there is no space in a book of this sort to discuss the problems connected with the Freudian view, one point could perhaps be usefully made. Freud himself only regarded a latent explanation of action in terms of the Unconscious as applicable in a set of clearly defined cases. He described these cases in terms of three criteria (1914):

(a) They must be faulty within normal limits—e.g., knocking a precious ink stand off the desk by mistake.

(b) They must evince the character of momentary and temporary disturbance. The same actions must have been performed more correctly previously, or we must rely on ourselves to perform them more correctly. If corrected by others we must recognize the truth of the correction.

(c) If the action is perceived as faulty, the agent must be unaware of its motivation and explain it through inattention, or attribute it to accident. These criteria do not surely delineate the kinds of situation which the caseworker has in mind when he regards some overt action as masking some latent wish or desire, as masking what the client 'really wants'. The actions described by Freud as amenable to this sort of explanation hardly count as actions at all. As Peters says (1960, p. 11): 'Freud only intended to explain by reference to unconscious mental processes cases where the purposive rule-following model of social behaviour breaks down.' This hardly seems to be the case with the caseworker's clients. A particular client may not happen to follow certain socially established rules, but this does not mean that his actions fall under one of the three rubrics laid down by Freud, unless one wishes to say that all socially deviant behaviour has the character of being accidental. If this were accepted then again it would conflict with respect for persons because it would deny the possibility of agency to social deviants. It is doubtful, then, whether any knowledge could justify any tendency on the part of caseworkers to espouse a positive theory of freedom, quite apart from general conceptual difficulties involved.

Individuality and morality

As the argument of this chapter has tried to make clear, casework theory seems to be committed to a strong conception of the individual. It conceives him in terms of a set of concepts such as respect for persons, acceptance and self-direction. What kind of conception of morality is appropriate to an individual conceived in these terms? It would seem, if the argument of this chapter is correct, that morality, to recommend itself to individuals understood in these terms, will have to be a matter for rational discussion and assent, and that this assent must be personal and individual. Moral principles and obligations must be thought out and accepted by free individuals. The difficulty here, however, is with the person who might reject generally accepted moral principles or who might perhaps fail to fulfil certain obligations incumbent upon him. How to approach an individual in this kind of situation is a central difficulty and cause of tension in casework theory. On the one hand, the theory stresses individuality; on the other, it also stresses the relationship between the individual and social morality.

Social morality and the standpoint of the individual

Caseworkers are concerned professionally not with the relationship between man and society as a whole, but rather with the way in which social claims and obligations impinge upon a man in the form of a particular social role, or nexus of such roles. Roles involve standards and norms, and the client of the social worker, whether he is voluntary or whether he has been committed to his care by the courts, has a problem which concerns his social function, his relationship to the standards implicit in and tied to these social roles. Moffett summarizes these points well (1968, p. 5):

A convenient general way of looking at the problems which come to casework agencies is in terms of a role. 'Role' is a sociological term denoting the way in which society has invested socially important activities with standardized obligations and rights, and people come to think in terms of roles and measure themselves against them. Anyone acts in a number of different roles at appropriate times. . . . Most of the problems coming to a social caseworker are largely concerned with one or another breakdown in the performance of roles, and are actually considered problems because their behaviour goes against the norms of society.

This account does justice to the fact that there is something which can be called social morality, which is not detached and amorphous, but rather discrete, and analysable into the norms which are attached to the performance of certain role functions in society. The philosophical problem here is the correct view of the relationship between the socially accepted standards which are attached to certain performances and the principles, ideas, beliefs and decisions of the individuals who actually perform in these roles. This is a problem for social caseworkers and not just academic theorists, in that the former is supposed to be committed to the values attached to individuals which we have already discussed. The problem for the caseworker is how individuals considered in terms of these concepts can be helped by him to come to accept the standards implicit in their social roles, for this is surely the central problem for casework. Perlman (1953, pp. 130-1) argues that:

> The problem which a client brings to a social agency is perceived by him to be a problem in his social adjustment. It may be caused by a breakdown of normal sources of social sustenance, or it may be caused by the malfunctioning of the person himself, but in each case the client sees and feels his problem in terms of social maladjustment because it makes itself known to him as he plays his social role. . . . The person in interaction with some problematic aspect of his social reality is the focus of the caseworker's concerns.

The understanding of this relationship does not take place in the void, however, in that casework itself has concepts to contribute to the understanding of the relationship; concepts related to the individual and to society. The problem is whether these concepts are adequate to the understanding of man in society. Certainly tension between these concepts has been felt by casework practitioners, particularly those whose agency seems clearly committed to the maintainance of certain socially accepted standards, and may indeed have a statutory duty to maintain them. Both Winnicott and Pollard have written of the difficulties here for a probation officer working within the conceptual framework of casework theory. Winnicott makes a particular point about the difficulty which a probation officer experiences in his attempt to uphold the standards of a society with a client committed to him by the courts and with whom the officer is supposed to do casework, which implies the capacity of the client for self-direction. Winnicott (Younghusband, 1967, p. 108):

> When a child or an adult commits an offence of a certain degree and kind he brings into action the machinery of the law. The probation officer who is asked to do casework with the client feels that he ought to apply

techniques implying the casework principle of self-determination, but he loses everything if he forgets his relationship to his agency and the court. . . .

The issue has been posed by Pollard in more general terms, which are applicable to any casework agency. Pollard (1962, p. 8):

The tension between the 'One and the many' in social work presents so complex a problem that the profession can hardly, it seems, develop their study of its two poles simultaneously. On the one hand there is the individual, who basically cannot be helped against his real wish . . . and on the other hand there is society, chiefly embodied in the agency which is part of the reality of the client's situation.

In order to facilitate the analysis of this problem two models will be examined. Both are extreme. One is the Existentialist model of the individual and his relationship to his social roles, the other the Idealist view of the relationship. The Existentialist regards role morality as sub-human and a form of bad faith. The Idealist regards the individual outside his social roles as a vicious abstraction. The weak points of both of these theories might well indicate the kinds of area in which an appropriate theory may be found.

Role morality: an Existentialist critique

The Existentialist, of whom I shall take J. P. Sartre as representative, is the philosopher who takes human freedom and self-direction seriously. He does so because in his view God does not exist, consequently there is no such thing as a necessary human nature. A nature can only exist when someone has a conception of it, and this is not so with mankind because the only person who could have a conception of man's essential nature would be God.

37

Man has no essence, no nature. His existence precedes his essence, that is, he exists in the world and builds his character or his nature through his own decisions. Because man has no set nature, no essence to fulfil in the world, no institution, no specific form of society, no particular moral code is necessary for man. Man has what Hegel might call 'the infinite negativity of spirit', that is to say, he can deny the value and the facticity of everything which is *given* in the world, in society, in morality and institutions. This freedom consists in stepping back from his role obligations which are conventionally accepted, and making up his own mind on moral matters, but at the same time it leads to anguish, because when a man chooses something in the world, and regards it as having value, there is no way of validating or supporting his choice. There is no authority which can be appealed to, and the agent has to take responsibility for the choices which he makes. To live authentically, that is to say, in full and serious knowledge of the contingency of the world and of human institutions, is to live in anguish. Most people are afraid of freedom, preferring to live in a state of bad faith, to live inauthentically, because they will not face the fact of contingency, the terrifying realization that there is no need to play a particular role or indeed any role unless one chooses. It would seem to follow from this that to help individuals to adjust to the claims of their social roles is to encourage bad faith. The following comment by Sartre on Idealist philosophy could be adopted with little change as a comment on social casework from the Existentialist point of view (1955, pp. 220-1):

> The possibility of rising above the situation is precisely what we call freedom. . . . Idealism deceives man in that it binds him with rights and duties already given: it conceals from him his power to blaze his own path.

Most people who read Sartre, particularly if they have

some acquaintance with the work of a sociologist such as Durkheim, will argue against him that his picture of human life is totally unrealistic. Men, it can be argued, need the discipline which comes from social morality. They need to be identified with the norms attached to particular social roles; they cannot stand on their feet in the way in which Sartre suggests. Durkheim attempted to show that the loosening of social bonds, of role identification, leads to a state of moral rootlessness which he calls *anomie* : a state which Durkheim argued was a major cause of suicide. To this the Existentialist would reply that the person who commits suicide merely shows that he is incapable of living an authentic human life. Sartre and Durkheim would probably agree on the facts, that the loosening of social bonds does lead to moral rootlessness, but each would take up different positions with regard to the facts. Sartre would approve of this situation because there are no real moral roots, and to believe that there are is an example of bad faith. Durkheim would regard this as a situation to be avoided. Men are not capable of being the moral monarchs of all they survey, as in Sartre's view. Casework surely allies itself with Durkheim in this dispute, in that it regards a failure in role performance as a *problem*, and not a sign that men are growing up and becoming more mature. The fully mature person is one who accepts, who is integrated with, the standards attached to his roles. Most caseworkers would agree with the comment of Dorothy Emmet on the Existentialist analysis of role morality (1966, p. 155):

Are we left then with an antithesis between role behaviour on the one hand with its legal and moral regulations which Sartre says evade the full freedom and responsibility of the individual, and on the other hand a purely personal morality, free, spontaneous, unbound by rules? The trouble with this antithesis is that it hardly comes to grips with social morality, and whether we like it or not, social morality impinges on our lives most of the time. We had much better recognize and respect the fact that, as Aristotle remarked, he that could live apart from society might be a beast or a God but not a human being.

Existentialism fails because it neither recognizes nor does justice to the facts of our social situation. But it will be argued that it would be a mistake for the caseworker to dismiss the insights which it has. In particular it will be argued that the possibility of role distance, of stepping back from one's obligations, is a necessary condition of holding the central casework concepts and in particular of respect for persons and acceptance.

Social morality: the Idealist approach

Sartre, as we have seen, criticizes the Idealist philosopher for insisting upon the centrality of role fulfilment in human life. The Existentialist sees morality and freedom essentially in terms of decision, choice and commitment. The Idealist on the contrary sees it more in the fulfilment of social obligations, and he regards the individual who stands back from his social roles, and who stands behind them as a shadowy abstraction. The *locus classicus* of this kind of approach to social morality is *Ethical Studies* by F. H. Bradley (1962), and in particular Essay V, 'My Station and Its Duties'. In this essay Bradley presents an extremely trenchant critique of the concept of the individual, particularly as this concept occurs in the work of the utilitarians, a philosophical movement fully committed to individualism. Society is not, in Bradley's view, a collection of free self-directing individuals, held together either through illusion, inertia or contract; rather society moulds individuals, it gives them conceptions of morality and ideals. Without ideals, morality and culture, all of which are social products, there would be no individuality or freedom. There is no such thing as the bare individual with his own capacities which he can develop, as the existentialists assert, by free acts of choice—acts which are inauthentic if they are performed in terms of given modes of culture and morality. Rather Bradley argues (p. 172):

He grows up in an atmosphere of general custom, his life widens out from one little world to other higher worlds, and he apprehends through different stations the whole in which he lives and has lived. Is he now to try to develop his individuality, his self which is not the same as other selves? Where is it? What is it? Where can he find it? The soul within him is saturated, is filled, is qualified by, it has assimilated, has got its substance, has built itself up from, it is one and the same life as the universal life, and if he turns against this he turns against himself.

As Emmet says, the essay is a polemic against the individualist who thinks that he has no duties except those which he has freely thought out and assumed for himself. Morality is not to be attained by accepting only those duties which one can justify to oneself, but rather living up to the standards implicit in one's form of life, one's social position, one's social role. To wish to be better than the world, that is to say the world ready to hand in social morality, is already to be on the threshold of immorality.

This powerful critique of individualism has received a recent stimulus from the work of the sociologist Erving Goffman (1968). In the two works cited, Goffman denies that the 'self' or the person is anything over and above the nexus of social roles which he plays. He is concerned to argue against what he calls attempts 'to make the world safe from sociology', and the thesis that an individual is not capable of being analysed into this particular role performances would be a clear case of such a tendency.

It has been argued that the Sartrian thesis is too extreme: we cannot really make sense of his conception of the individual and his powers, because it so contradicts the way in which we do feel *constrained* by social practices, and *obliged* by relationships over which we have no control. It might also be argued that an anti-individualistic thesis, as argued by Bradley and Goffman, is too extreme. It could, in general, be argued that we should keep the concept of an individual who stands apart from his social roles. We do need the notion of role distance, otherwise if a person is identifiable with his roles, and if roles relate to socially useful activities, then it is possible that a person will be treated as a thing, as a means to another's end, or as a means to society's ends. A man may be shifted from one role to another without any concern about the way in which this change of role or station will affect the inner man, because there is no inner man to be affected, there is no individual who stands 'behind' his roles.

It could also be argued that such a thesis controverts what we have seen is the basic casework value, namely respect for persons. It is part of the concept of respect for persons that a man is respected in terms of the *human* capacities which he has, not in terms of his social position or his social role. In Goffman's view this must be a value which is devoid of sense, there is no such inner man that can be respected, there is nothing which transcends the performance of certain roles. So too the concept of acceptance could not really make sense of such a view. A person who adopted the point of view of either Bradley or Goffman could not make sense of the following quotation from Biestek (1961, p. 72):

Acceptance is the principle of action wherein the caseworker perceives and deals with the client as he really is, including his strengths and weaknesses, his congenial and uncongenial qualities, his positive and negative feelings, his constructive and destructive attitudes and behaviour, maintaining all the while a sense of the client's *innate* dignity and personal worth. . . . The human person has *intrinsic* value. He has innate dignity and worth, basic rights and needs.

This presupposes what Goffman denies: the inner redoubt theory of the self that there is an inner man who is the bearer of dignity and worth irrespective of the roles which he plays and the manner and style of his performance.

It would seem then that neither the Existentialist nor the proponent of the kind of view under discussion can provide an adequate model of the relationship between man and society, or at least not one which can accommodate the basic casework concepts and attitudes. The Existentialist must fail for the caseworker because the caseworker must see difficulties in social functioning as *problems*, and not as *signs of maturity and freedom*. The view of the Idealist cannot be adequate either, because it seems difficult to accommodate the casework values of respect for persons, and acceptance. It is necessary to preserve the concept of the individual who stands 'behind' his social role, but this does not entail that the individual is the basic category in terms of which we should look at modes of social life, as the Existentialist maintains. The Existentialist is incorrect in so far as he thinks that man can exist apart from his social roles, whereas the Idealist philosopher and the so-called 'dramatic' sociologists such as Goffman are also incorrect in thinking that the individual is totally absorbed by his roles. As Emmet says (1966, p. 132):

. . . a morality simply of direct I-Thou relationships cannot take account of the host of indirect personal relations in which we stand to people nor the impersonal element which arises even in a personal morality,

43

and *a fortiori* in the morality of official institutional relations. A purely personalist morality since it cannot come to terms with these must abandon them to anarchy (which is unrealistic) or to external regulation which may be all too realistic.

Man in Society: The analysis of The Long Revolution

The Existentialist and the Idealist talk in a hypostasized manner; the Existentialist of the 'individual' and the Idealist of 'society'. In so doing they show that they are a part of that shared tradition of concepts and descriptions to which Raymond Williams has drawn attention. Casework practice seems to cast doubt on this hypostasization, and it might be argued that there is a tension between experience and the description of it which necessitates transcending these categories to new forms of description in terms of which the caseworker may be able to understand the client's relationship to society and his own relationship to both. If the categories of 'individual' and 'society' are not appropriate to an understanding of our social experience, then casework theory needs to be recast in terms which do reflect and illuminate the experience which we have in our social encounters.

One point which militates against breaking out of the strait jacket of the 'individual'/'society' dichotomy to new forms of description is the influence of Freud on casework theory. It might be argued that Freud had provided a scientific sanctification of the conceptual status quo. As Williams points out (1966, p. 96):

> For Freudian theory assumes a basic division between the individual and society. . . . Man, the 'bare human being' has certain fundamental drives which are also fundamentally antisocial. . . . Man as a 'bare human being' is thus fundamentally alienated from society, and the best that can be hoped for is a reasonably adjusted

balance between the conflicting needs of the individual and society.

However, as an attempt will be made in the penultimate chapter to show the possibility of transcending the Freudian picture, this influence will be left out of account in the current discussion of the important new insights which Williams gives into the nature of our social experience.

Williams rejects the Existentialist analysis of the relationship between man and society because it visualizes the relationship in terms of *subject* and *servant*. The individual, when he is inauthentic, in the Existentialist view is the servant of society. He sees society as trying to impose a strait jacket of culture and morality on the individual—a view which does not do justice to the fact that we experience ourselves as *members* of society, not merely as subjects of its dictates. The Idealist, too, is mistaken because he clearly sees the relationship in terms of subject and servant—as the very title of Bradley's essay makes clear. This view does profound violence to man's deepest instincts (Williams, 1966, p. 105):

> The servant, may come to identify himself with the way of life that is determining him; he may even consciously think of himself as a member. . . . Yet at many levels of his life, and particularly in certain situations such as solitude and age, the discrepancy between the role the individual is playing and his actual sense of himself will become manifest either consciously or in terms of some physical or emotional disturbance.

Williams argues that there is a need for a more complex description in terms of which we can understand the response of members to a society. There is a need to get beyond concepts such as conformity, non-conformity, adjustment, maladjustment, integration, disintegration, because these tend to presuppose a unitary relationship or lack of it between the individual on the one hand and society on the other. In fact, however, there are many and varied relationships or lack of relationships between a person and his environment. Williams, for example, distinguishes the *member*—the person who feels very clearly identified with his social experience, who finds the way of life of his community deeply expressive of his own character; the *subject*—the person who feels that society is repressive and does not feel at all identified with it, but who cannot sustain himself outside of it; the *exile*—the person who does not fight against the form of life in his society, but leaves it; the *rebel*—the person who fights aggressively against the social experience which he has, but fights from within society; the *vagrant*—the man who drifts within the way of life but 'finds its purposes meaningless and its values irrelevant'. As there are different relationships to society, so society appears under a different description to those who are related to it in different ways. The member feels that society is a community to which he feels closely tied; the servant feels that society is an establishment in which he has a place with attendant duties, while to the rebel, society appears as a system of repression. There is no pure individual, because the individual always has some particular relationship to society, and there is no 'society' as such, rather different ways of having and interpreting social experience.

If these arguments are valid, then their relevance for casework seems to be that the caseworker should not pose the tension in his professional concern as that between the individual and society because the descriptions do not take account of the complexities of relationships. Casework needs far more sophisticated tools. In so far as a great deal of casework experience will be concerned with those people who have some problem in their social functioning, then it would seem a prerequisite of effective casework to identify the particular mode of social malfunctioning—to understand the descriptions in terms of which the client sees and interprets his social experience; whether he sees it as a vagrant, a servant, a rebel, etc. The casework aim will not be to help to change the description of experience as such, because without changing the mode of social experience in question, this would be both dishonest and futile. The aim must be to help the client by various therapeutic techniques to come to experience his way of life in a different manner, namely as a member. It may be, of course, that this cannot be done because only a community may have members, and it may be that the *society* in question cannot be experienced by anyone authentically as a *community*. To help a person to feel a member of a society which could not be really experienced as a community would be to do violence to the individual's personality.

It is clearly possible for this to happen. An individual may acquiesce of his own volition or as a result of therapy in a way of life which fails to correspond to or satisfy his deepest needs. He will obey authorities which he does not personally accept and carry out social functions which have no meaning for him, even feel and think in ways so foreign to his actual desires that damage will be done to his own being—often deep emotional disorders, often physical damage to his organic processes.

If the casework aim is to help people to experience their social life as members of a community then clearly we need some conception of what a community is and what kind of experience a man will be able to have as a member. The problem of delineating what a truly human community could be has been a concern of political theory since the decline of the Greek city-state which has often been taken by political philosophers as the paradigm of community life. The next chapter will attempt to show that any answer to this question must be moral or political, and it will do this by arguing that the concept of *mental health* cannot, as has often been thought, provide some kind of scientific criterion whereby the concept of a community, of an adequate object of human adjustment can be delineated. Casework, then, in so far as its aims coincide with what has been said in the last section of this chapter, is involved in seeking an answer to one of the oldest questions of political thought.

3

Community and mental health

'Mental health and illnesses are new words for describing moral values.'

(Szasz, 1968)

'Adaptation to what? To society? To a world gone mad?'

(R. D. Laing, 1967)

In the previous chapter I indicated that the aims of casework might well be considered in terms of an effort to help a person to become a *member* of a *community*. That is to say, to help the person to find his self-realization and the fulfilment of his deepest needs in a community which is appropriate for this. As it stands, however, this seems perhaps to be too self-consciously moral an end, and in this context it is interesting to look at the concept of mental health to see if this can provide a more scientific conception of the casework aim. As it is conventionally understood, mental health seems to be concerned with the problem of individual self-realization in a particular environment. First of all a survey of definitions of mental health will be given, followed by a similar survey of casework aims, and the relationship which is thought to hold between self-realization and environment will be discussed.

Mental health: self-realization and environment

The following definitions are, I would argue, representative

49

of the kind of understanding of the concepts of mental health which we have at present.

The term normal or healthy can be defined in two ways. Firstly, from the standpoint of functioning society one could call a person normal or healthy if he is able to fulfil the social roles which he is to take in that given society. Secondly, from the standpoint of the individual we look upon health or normalcy as the optimum of growth and happiness in the individual (Eaton, 1951, p. 85).

Let us define mental health as the adjustment of human beings to the world and to each other with a maximum of effectiveness and happiness (Eaton, 1951, p. 85).

A human being in good mental health is capable of positive emotional, social and intellectual adjustment to his environment and he is able to establish harmonious relationships with other people (U.N.O., 1955, p. 84).

The healthy personality is one which functions more or less perfectly in its cultural milieu (Davis, 1938, p. 59).

Mental health . . . is influenced by both biological and social factors. It is not a static condition but subject to variations and fluctuations of degree; The committee's conception implies the capacity in an individual to form harmonious relationships with others and to participate in, or to contribute constructively to, changes in his social and physical environment. . . . It implies in addition an individual whose personality has developed in a way which enables his potentially conflicting instinctive drives to find harmonious expression in the full realization of his potentialities (W.H.O., 1951, p. 4).

In all of these definitions, a dual emphasis is to be discerned. On the one hand, the individual and his capacities which demand realization; on the other, the society in which the person lives. The relationship between the two is ideally conceived as one in which self-realization is to be found in being a full member of a community. If the concept of mental health is scientific then it might provide some empirical validation for what in the previous chapter, was argued could be seen as the central casework aim. This dual emphasis, and the image of man's relationship to his environment which is involved in the concept of mental health can also be perceived in conventional characterizations of casework aims.

Community and casework

In this exposition of the aims of social casework, the author is indebted to the work of Swithun Bowers (Kasius, 1950). In his paper Bowers assembled over thirty definitions of casework, a large number of which stress and exemplify the points made here. Most of these definitions involve his two-sided emphasis on individual self-realization and environmental adaptation. It might be appropriate to look initially at the definition of casework aims proposed by Mary Richmond who stands at the beginning of the current tradition of casework. Mary Richmond writes (1930, p. 477) that social work involves: 'Those processes which develop the personality through adjustment, effected individual by individual, between men and society.' Here at the very beginning of contemporary casework this dual emphasis is expressed; that casework is concerned with the development of the personality in and through a social context. The definition which Bowers (Kasius, 1950, p. 127) advocates illustrates the same point:

> Casework is an art in which the knowledge of the science of human relationships, and skill in relationships are used to mobilize capacities in the individual and resources in the community appropriate for better adjustment.

The same emphasis is to be found outside Anglo-American

casework theory. Corgiat, an Italian theorist, writes (1954, p. 73):

> Social service aims to orientate the individual in reference to his own task in his daily life, his relationships with members of his family or community, his health, his work, his leisure time, in order that he may find within himself the elements for the alleviation of grievance and for his own improvement.

The salient feature of all these definitions is the same as that noticed in the definitions of mental health, namely the emphasis upon the individual's development in an environment which facilitates it. Again the appropriate language in terms of which to describe this relationship between the individual and his social environment is that of a member of a community. It will be remembered that Williams defined this relationship as one in which the person feels very closely identified with his social experience, and who finds the way of life of his community deeply expressive of his own character.

The problem then is whether the concept of mental health can provide any empirical basis for this kind of aim, or whether, as Szasz comments in the quotation at the head of this chapter, mental health is a contemporary way of making moral judgements sound more cogent by giving them the backing of some kind of scientific respectability. It will in fact be the argument of the next part of this chapter that the concept of mental health is an incorrigibly moral concept. It will further be argued that the definitions given are too vague at crucial points, particularly over the way in which the relation between self-realization and the community is envisaged. In order to facilitate the analysis of this last point the problems will be set out here in a schematic manner.

(a) It might be argued that there is only a contingent relationship between the individual's ability to fulfil his deepest needs and the particular kind of society in which he lives. Self-realization on this view is consistent with any sort of society because it is an asocial thing.

(b) alternatively it might be argued that in fact self-realization is only possible within a socio-cultural context, because there is no self to be realized outside such a context. The content of human capacities and powers is given by society;

(c) against this it might be argued that self-realization in the sense of the development of truly human capacities cannot be achieved within certain sorts of society, because these societies are too repressive in one way or another. That is to say that only *some societies* can be experienced as *communities*. Social malfunctioning is a result of the state of society rather than some fault of the individuals who are maladjusted. The problems inherent in understanding the true nature of the relationship between self-realization and environment as envisaged in the definitions of mental health which have been discussed are well summarized by Marcuse (1969, p. 203):

> Either one defines 'personality' and 'individuality' within the established form of civilization, in which case then realization is, for the vast majority, tantamount to successful adjustment. Or one defines them in terms of their transcending content including their socially denied potentialities . . . in this case realization would imply transgression beyond the established form of civilization to radically new modes of personality and individuality incompatible with the prevailing ones.

If casework aims can be understood in terms of the promotion of mental health then it might be argued that casework is in fact a scientific practice. Its problems, namely social maladjustment and attendant difficulties, might be specified in scientific terms—in terms of mental health or illness, and its techniques might certainly rank as scientific.

53

Casework as applied science

It might be argued that the caseworker is in an analogous position to the medical practitioner in that the aim of both professions is to promote health or to cure some kind of ill, and in that casework stands in the same relationship to a corpus of theoretical knowledge (sociology, psychology and social administration) as medicine does in relationship to the various branches of medical science. Casework, like medicine, is the disinterested application of a body of theoretical knowledge to the solution of some problem which is specifiable in descriptive terms. This clearly seems to be implied in Bowers's definition (Kasius, 1950): 'Casework is an art in which the knowledge of the science of human relationships and skill in relationship are used to mobilize capacities in the individual and resources in the community appropriate for better adjustment.' The analogy between casework and medicine has been used in the caseworkers' struggle for recognition as professional people, but, whatever the polemical point of the analogy and its usefulness in the internal politics of the social work profession, it should be considered on its merits. If the concept of mental health does prove in fact to be morally and politically committed, then it seems that this kind of analogy which would make casework a form of applied science must break down.

As the definitions quoted above stand, they do seem to involve some kind of moral and political commitments, and it is difficult to see how any modification of the definitions could weaken these. The emphasis in mental health theory upon self-realization through adjustment or integration into the social environment in which individuals live does seem to involve a commitment to the adequacy of that to which the individual is to be helped to adjust. If this is so then the question 'Adaptation to what?' posed by Laing at the head of this chapter seems to be relevant. Barbara Wootton makes the point in a less extreme manner (1967, p. 218):

> In the literature of mental health generally, this concept of adjustment is particularly prominent. Fine phrases cannot however obscure the fact that adjustment means adjustment to a particular culture or to a set of institutions; and so to conceive adjustment and maladjustment in medical terms is in effect to identify health with the ability to come to terms with that culture or with the institutions—be they totalitarian methods of government, the dingy culture of an urban slum, the contemporary English law of marriage, or what I have elsewhere called the standards of an 'acquisitive, competitive, hierarchical, envious society'.

This point has been discerned even by those who are ardent advocates of the concept. For example Soddy argues (1962, p. 70): 'Mental health is associated with principles dependent upon the prevailing religion or ideology of the community concerned.' The person who wishes to use the concept of mental health in the understanding of his activity seems at this point to be caught on the horns of a dilemma. On the one hand, he could agree with Wootton's view and accept the consequences, namely that he is committed to a view that social deviance, if not definable in terms of mental illness, is at least a sign of it; this clearly implies that the existing state of society is something to which people ought to conform. Alternatively, he could adopt the view that only some societies and cultures are appropriate environments for human self-realization, or in Williams's terminology, only some societies can be experienced as communities. Both of these alternatives imply some kind of moral commitment of a conservative or of a radical nature. This point has been clearly brought out by Donnison (1955, p. 349):

It is generally agreed that burst pipes and disease are undesirable. Physicians and plumbers are therefore employed to prevent or cure ills without having to think much about the purpose or social consequences of their prescriptions. The ends to be attained and the areas of competence are both fairly clear. But in social work this is not so. There is no generally understood state of 'social health' towards which all people strive; our disagreements on this question form the subject matter of politics the world over.

(Of course the force of this argument with reference to medicine has been weakened recently; the ability to keep more and more people alive for longer and longer, and the current vogue for organ transplantation, do give substance to the argument that in fact the practice of medicine is not merely applied science, but is morally engaged.)

The same point is made with greater force by J. Wilson (1965, p. 36):

Whereas we can reasonably say that what is physically 'normal' in the sense of 'statistically average', is often also 'normal' in the sense of 'healthy'. We cannot say this about what is supposed to be mentally 'normal'. Throughout the world, every society has wanted its individuals to be active, able to run, not to suffer pain, to live long and be strong etc. But the demands made on a person in respect of his mental 'normalcy' vary very widely; unlike physical health, what is regarded as mentally 'normal' differs from age to age and clime to clime.

The relativity of mental health

To take up the last point made by Wilson: if mental health is at least partly defined in terms of self-realization in a particular community, in terms of normal functioning in a society, then it seems to make the concept entirely relative and tied to a particular culture. This means that there can be no diagnosis of a society itself, its standards, norms and values as being mentally unhealthy, or not conducive to mental health, since mental health is defined as adjustment, integration and self-realization within these standards and norms. This is only apparently an exclusively theoretical difficulty. Some people have wanted to argue that the standards and norms of some primitive cultures are signs of profound mental disorder, others have wanted to argue the point somewhat nearer home, and in fact classify contemporary western societies as mentally sick. A clear case of the former would be Emmet's discussion of the Dobu tribe. She writes (1966, pp. 102-3):

> Indeed the description of Dobu society reads like a description of a paranoiac society in which everyone may be under suspicion. If you plant a tree, you put a curse laying a horrible disease on anyone who steals the fruit; but a thief will put a still more horrible counter-curse on you. A thief, you may say, is up to no good anyway; but even in the intimate relations of marriage, each spouse goes in continual fear of sorcery or witchcraft from the other. It is indeed a society permeated by envy, hatred, malice and all uncharitableness.

If, however, the concept of mental health and its converse is defined in terms of adequate functioning within one's cultural milieu, then it is difficult to see how one could justify talking in the way in which Emmet does. She clearly wants to argue that some ways of life are better than others, in terms of the development of human potentialities and powers. Some societies facilitate this more than others. But, if mental health is to be defined in social terms, then it seems that it cannot be the kind of critical tool which Emmet requires it to be, nor can it be the central instrument in what might be called the critical theory of Western society in the ambitious way in which Fromm (1963) and Marcuse (1969) wish. Fromm and

Marcuse want to argue that contemporary Western societies are sick, and to function adequately in such a sick society is to exhibit the same kind of symptoms of mental ill health as Emmet regards the adjusted, unprotesting Dobu to be exhibiting. A great deal then depends upon the way in which we want to take the concept of mental health, whether we do want to define it in social terms, or whether we want to give it some kind of meaning which totally transcends a particular cultural and social milieu. These problems will be discussed later in the chapter. Some preliminary distinctions must be drawn before the questions posed here can be answered.

Mental health and the concept of human nature

'Our conception of mental health depends upon our conception of human nature' (Fromm, 1963).

The same pattern of argument can be applied to the other aspect of mental health; the conception of developing the human personality, maximizing human powers. It might be argued that if the notion of realizing human capacities is a central part of the definition of the concept of mental health, then again it is inevitably involved in some kind of social and moral commitment. In the first place, it might be argued that there is no kind of expertise which can be used for deciding what really constitutes a human potentiality. The psychologist cannot take us very far along the road to deciding what the basic human potentialities are, in the void, outside a particular form of life. The only kinds of concepts which might be formulated in this abstract way are purely formal, for example that men are capable of reason, that they are able to act and are not just acted upon, that men are rule-following animals, and so on. This is about as far as can be gone in elucidating the concept of human potentialities without specifying the particular form of life in question. The concepts here are purely formal (cf. Peters, 1968). They can only be filled in by reference to societies and the paradigms of human nature presupposed in those societies. If this point is correct, that apart from a few very formal concepts, the concept of human nature, and its content are socially given, then it might be argued that there is again a commitment implicit in the concept, to the standards of human thought and action in a particular society. This commitment leads to the same kinds of complications as were discussed in the previous section. Furthermore, a general point which was made in an earlier chapter is relevant here, namely that no descriptions of the standards implicit in a society, or of the recognized ends of life in that society, can entail that these are desirable ends of human endeavour, or that people ought to adopt them.

In so far, then, as the aims of casework can be understood in terms of the concept of mental health, it seems that casework is morally engaged in some way or other. Mental health is not a purely scientific concept; rather, as Szasz points out, it is a new way of making moral judgements about the relationship between people and their social environment. The mentally healthy person is the one who finds the way of life in his community deeply related to his own springs of action, his own patterns of thought and endeavour. The mentally healthy person is clearly one who, in Williams's terminology, experiences his society as a community. But to say that this is the kind of model of social relationships behind the concept of mental health in fact raises a whole host of moral and social problems: can any society be experienced as a community (or in the language of mental health: is any society an appropriate object of human adjustment?) If not, how can we tell those societies which can be understood as communities and those which cannot? (How can we decide which societies are appropriate settings for the development of mental health?) How can a person be led, helped, or induced to feel that he is a member of a community? (By what techniques can self-realization be achieved?) These are parallel problems, and they cannot be answered solely by empirical investigation. It might be interesting to speculate why the language of mental health seems to have taken the place of a great deal of moral language. It might be a result of the problems of finding some validity for moral judgements, whereas the language of mental health sounds scientific and is therefore more acceptable. It gives a scientific veneer to moral judgements. It might be a result of the fact that with the growth of permissiveness, moral language has lost most of its cutting edge, yet there is a need to appraise, control and classify the behaviour of people, and the language of mental health is more cogent and, therefore, a more efficient way of doing this than the language of morals.

The social and political commitments of casework

The next section of this chapter will examine the exact nature of the moral and social commitments which have been indicated. Whether we take a totally moral view of casework and argue that its fundamental aim of helping people to come to terms with society in fact presupposes a model of the relationship between man and society in which the man is seen as a member and the society a community; or whether we take what seemed to be a more 'scientific' view and understand casework aims in terms of the development of mental health, the commitments have only been indicated and not so far analysed.

If it is argued that 'self-realization' and the development of 'human personality' on the one hand, and 'adjustment' and 'integration' to a particular social environment on the other hand, are in fact notionally distinct, then it is possible that a conflict can occur in a particular context as to which concern is basic to the caseworker. Again, this is not theorician's dilemma. For example, Pollard argues (1962, p. 8) that the question is: 'When a choice between a society's needs and those of an individual become inevitable for the caseworker, he must know which to prefer.' Whether in a particular case the caseworker should allow, or help an individual to perform some kind of action which he regards as necessary to the development of the client's personality and conducive to his maturity, and which is not at the same time in accordance with the legal code or commonly accepted standards of morality, clearly might pose a difficult question for caseworkers. Some theorists think that the answer can be given in wholly general terms. Biestek (1961, p. 94) writes: 'First the caseworker because he is a social worker, has a social responsibility: he is the agent, a representative of the community; whether employed in a public or private agency. By profession he is necessarily allied with social, legal and moral good.' Most caseworkers would, I think, argue that the situation is not altogether as straightforward as Biestek suggests. The answer to the question may well depend upon the function and the status of the agency in question. Some casework functions such as those performed by the probation officer are statutory, and it might be argued that there is an explicit contradiction involved in the probation officer's facilitating an action which would be against the law, even in the unlikely case of thinking that such an action might promote his client's maturity. In these circumstances the agency itself seems to determine the answer to Pollard's question. In a voluntary agency the answer might not be so straightforward. Indeed the empirical evidence, such as it is, seems to confirm the kind of interpretation of the problem given here rather than

the blanket solution proposed by Biestek. Noel Timms
quotes the following examples (1968, p. 56):

> Only a quarter [of the caseworkers] were in favour of
> meeting the client's needs even if this required violating
> agency policy: 57% if this meant violating stated pro-
> fessional standards, and 95% if it meant violating com-
> munity expectations. 98% were in favour of action
> according to professional standards even if this meant
> violating community expectation.

This certainly shows the fallacy of Biestek's conceptual
approach to the problem—because caseworkers are *social*
workers they are *necessarily* allied to *social* norms and
standards. As Timms perceptively points out (p. 57): 'If,
for example, 95% of the workers were in favour of meet-
ing a client's needs even if this involved violating community expectation, should we not reconsider the view
. . . of social work as "society's conscience"?' A strong-
minded theorist might argue that these workers are in fact
misguided in thinking that clients had any important needs
to fulfil which might contradict the paradigms of human
needs present in society's standards. Self-realization is
impossible outside of these standards. Man is a psycho-
social animal and on this view there can be no incom-
patibility between an individual's self-realization and the
environment in which he lives. There is necessary relationship between self-realization, in the sense of man's 'real
self' or his 'rational self', and society. As it stands this
thesis is not at all clear. It does not make clear whether
self-realization is attainable in any society or only some
societies. The existence of society is essential to the
actualization of human potentialities—but what sort of
society? An answer to this might be that the very existence of casework *specifies* the kind of society. It is a
common argument that certain concepts which are central
to casework activity presuppose the existence of a *demo-*

cratic society. So casework, the argument might run, is in fact upholding the view that self-realization is only possible within a democracy or, to revert again to Williams's terminology, only a democracy can be a community of which an individual can be a member. Democracy is a presupposition of casework because only in a democratic society can concepts such as respect for persons, self-direction, etc., have a meaning. This point is made very strongly, if rather uncritically, by Biestek (1961) and by Hamilton (1950, p. 7):

> Casework has an honourable record in our democracy and must play a significant role in any free society. That casework would be meaningless in any but a free society I am sure you agree, for casework postulates values in individual development for full socialized capacities.

Similarly Towle (1954, p. 364) writes:

> As the basic concepts and working principles of casework are presented and discussed, they are identified as old, in that they are the basic tenets of democracy as a way of life . . . we are concerned that social casework be a democratic helping process.

There are several points which can be made here. In the first place it is not at all clear, as we have seen in the previous chapter, that the meaning of these central concepts, which are taken to presuppose a democratic social order, are in practice what they seem to be in theory. It might be argued that self-direction is only possible in a democratic society, although the point is without serious difficulty (Berlin, 1969, pp. 129-131), but as was seen in the previous chapter the concept of self-direction tends to have an ambiguous meaning in casework theory, and in so far as it might imply a theory of positive freedom it is compatible with any form of *totalitarian* system. Furthermore, there is no ideal type of democracy, and it is difficult to be sure what does constitute a democratic government. Perhaps the verdict of an eminent political scientist is relevant here (Crick, 1964): 'Democracy is perhaps the most promiscuous word in the world of public affairs. She is everybody's mistress, and yet retains her magic even when a lover sees that her favours are being, in his light, shared by many another.' As Timms points out (1968, p. 6), the term democracy is itself problematic, and he cites MacPherson (1965) as showing that liberal democracy, communist and under-developed variants can all be legitimately described as democratic. In addition to the problem of the multiplicity of states which call themselves democracies there are many theories which are critical of the notion of democracy as applied to contemporary Western societies. The work of Mills (1956), Pareto (1966), and Bottomore (1966) makes the assertion that casework presupposes democracy appear somewhat glib and implausible. (For a clear and judicious account of the issues raised here reference can be made to Parry, 1969.) Unless some clear characterization can be given to the concept of democracy for advanced industrial societies— and such characterizations seem to be extremely vague see Bachrach, 1967 and Kariel, 1961), then this criterion is useless as a critical tool for differentiating between those societies which are appropriate objects of human adjustment and those which are not. It cannot provide a standard for deciding which societies can be understood as communities, as forms of social experience through which human personality may be realized and brought to maturity.

It could also be argued that a commitment to a democratic society does not remove the problems involved in social commitments of caseworkers. If the desirable ends of life and the standards of self-realization are set by the culture of that society, then, even if it is a democratic one, it might be that life in such a society would be extremely poor and stereotyped. In order to provide for the possibility of choice and change even quite radical social deviance must be allowed. Mill saw this as a central danger in the growth of democracy. In a fully democratic society, Mill argued, the political and social power would be wielded by the dominant social class which in a democracy he thought would be the working class. This would entail that the whole cultural milieu of society would be permeated with the ethos of working-class culture. If the standards of self-realization were taken from a democratic society then, unless the possibility for social deviance were allowed, these standards of self-realization might be of a very poor sort:

> The majority in any one society must consist of persons all standing in the same social position, and having in the main the same pursuits—namely unskilled manual labourers—and they would make a narrow, mean kind of human nature perpetual.

Of course, it is not necessary to sympathize with Mill's assessment of working-class culture in order to appreciate the point which he is trying to make. Mill had not the advantage of reading recent sociological reports on the nature and value of working-class culture. The point is still valid—a democratic society may just as easily impose a moral and cultural strait jacket on people as a totalitarian society. The merit of Mill's essay *On Liberty* is to show that the situation is no more tolerable for being based upon the standards of the majority.

A final point to be made about the thesis that casework presupposes a democratic social order is far more polemical and committed. The Marxist would argue that the caseworkers' use of concepts, such as respect for persons and self-direction, embodies a form of false consciousness. The caseworker claims that these concepts only have a meaning in a democratic society and therefore casework is committed to democracy. The Marxist will argue that, in the economic system which historically has been tied to the development of liberal democracy, namely capitalism, there is no place for the concept of what Biestek calls 'man's intrinsic value, his inalienable worth'. These concepts are merely ideological; they do not reflect anything about the way in which men are treated in that part of their life which determines the structure of the rest, namely their economic existence. There is, it is argued, no respect for persons in the capitalist system; indeed the worth and value of the human person is denied by that system. This is the kind of thesis argued with great moral fervour by Marx in his essay *Estranged Labour* (1844). Far from having dignity and respect in the capitalist system, man is alienated from his own species, from his own creative potentialities, and from his fellow men (1844, p. 108): 'In the sphere of political economy this realization of labour appears as the loss of realization for the workers; objectification as loss of the object and bondage to it; appropriation as estrangement and alienation'. In the capitalist system, work, which is the basic spring of action in man, the basic mode of his creativity, is transformed into slavery. Man does not work to satisfy basic human needs, namely the need to create and externalize himself; rather he has to work to satisfy the needs of the economic system. The same kind of criticism could be made of the caseworker's use of self-direction: people are not in fact free even in the apparent economic freedom brought by the affluent society. Their needs and wants are manipulated by the economic system in the shape of the copywriter. (For a powerful but controversial statement of this position see Marcuse, 1964.) Casework concepts, then, have only an ideological function in liberal democratic societies which are based upon the capitalist system.

66

If the arguments presented in this section have any validity, then it follows that the activity of social casework does not in itself constitute a critical standard in terms of which the possibility of a society being experienced as a community, as an environment within which human beings find their deepest needs satisfied, can be judged. The activity of casework does not impose any limitation on the kind of social experience which is necessary for human development. Biestek says (1961, p. 94):

> . . . the caseworker, because he is a social worker, has a social responsibility; he is an agent, a representative of the community whether employed in a public or a private agency. By profession he is necessarily allied with the social, legal and moral good.

Biestek, however, does not consider that this point of view raises problems since for him casework values only have meaning within a particular community, a community which is a democracy based upon a belief in God. In the previous chapter an attempt was made to argue that the existence or the non-existence of God is irrelevant to the justification of the central casework values, and in this section of the chapter, I have argued that casework itself is compatible with any kind of social or political order. A deduction cannot be made from the activity of casework itself as to what kind of society is an appropriate object of human adjustment, or what kind of society can be experienced as a community.

If this point is admitted, then the following point made by Barbara Wootton becomes relevant. She discusses the problem in terms of mental health, but as we have seen, the development of mental health might be viewed as a casework aim (1967, p. 215): '. . . the dilemma is fundamental. In order to appreciate its quality, it may be helpful to consider how many of these definitions (of mental health) would allow a whole-hearted Nazi to qualify as a mentally healthy person in a Nazi-controlled society.' The Nazi finds his self-realization by coming to terms with and living through the social experience to hand in his society. Most people would want to argue with Marcuse at this point, however (1968, p. 251):

Is not the individual who functions normally, adequately and healthily as a citizen of a sick society—is not such an individual himself sick? And would not a sick society require an antagonistic concept of mental health, a meta-concept designating (and preserving) mental qualities which are tabooed, arrested, or distorted by the 'sanity' prevalent in the sick society? (For example, mental health equals the ability to live as a dissenter, to live a non-adjusted life.)

Indeed a similar point has been made by Soddy, who in general is not critical of the concept as it is conventionally understood (1962, pp. 75-6):

In the past and still today in some societies, adaptation to society has been highly valued . . . as a sign of mental health; and failure to adapt has been considered as a sign of mental ill health. There are occasions and situations in which from the point of view of mental health, rebellion and non-conformity are more important than social adaptation.

Implicit in both of these views is the assumption that on some occasions social deviance may be sanctioned in the interests of mental health. Or to put it in a manner which uses the same model, the experience of the rebel may be the authentic social experience in a society which has no claims to be a community. The problem is, as Szasz (De George, 1968) points out, what sort of criteria can be given for recognizing these situations. It is certainly assumed that such criteria are, in principle, obtainable, and even in the view of some people that these criteria may be scientific. For example, Thibaut (1943) argues that mental health conceived in terms of adjustment is certainly not an adequate concept, and he suggests that instead of helping non-conforming people, the rebels and the vagrants of a society, to come to terms with their cultural milieu, the emphasis should rather be upon a revision of the culture in the interests of mental health. The problem here is to try to answer the question: what sort of society is conducive to mental health? When, in fact, is the social deviant pointing towards a deep malaise in his environment, and gesturing towards new and better forms of social experience. Thibaut argues that it is not possible at the present time to give clear-cut answers to these questions, nor to specify precisely the social conditions which are in the interests of mental health, but he clearly considers that this is a scientific problem which can be solved by further research: 'This difficulty . . . is not insuperable, since the norm provides a conceptual orientation which by specific suggested researches can eventually describe the optimum conditions for collective adjustment.' In view of the argument so far, however, this scientific optimism may look somewhat ill-founded. The concept of mental health is intractably moral, and there can be no scientific answers to problems of value. If this kind of approach is allowed in principle—that is to say, if it is allowed that only some societies can be appropriate objects of human development, can be experienced as communities—then it would seem that on occasion casework might be socially subversive. If casework is in a society which *cannot* be a community, then the aims of casework will be frustrated unless the society is changed. The most that the caseworker could do in a society of this sort would be to help a person to become neither a rebel nor a vagrant, but rather the servant or subject in the society, and this clearly conflicts with respect for persons and self-direction.

It may be then, that in order to achieve their aim of

developing the human personality through adjustment and integration into social conditions, the caseworker is necessarily led to formulate a critical theory of society in order to facilitate the fulfilment of the basic aims of the profession. He needs to be able to formulate a concept of a truly human community which then will become a critical tool for interpreting the experience of people in his own society. Or to put the same point in the idiom of mental health, he must be able to formulate the concept of a healthy society in order to assess whether the society in which he does his casework can be conducive to the mental health of his clients. These problems are however central problems of social and political theory and casework is then in the thick of philosophical and ideological controversy. This is precisely the point made by Donnison which was quoted earlier (1955, p. 349): 'There is no generally understood state of social health towards which all men strive; our disagreements on this question form the subject matter of politics all the world over.' In the next section of the chapter some of the principles which might enter into a critical theory of society will be examined.

The possibility of a critical theory of society

The problem is this: part of the aim of social work is to promote mental health, or in the moral model which lies behind this concept, to help people to become members of a community; on the other hand, it is recognized that only some environments are conducive to mental health, that only some societies can be experienced as communities. The problem is to provide some kind of criteria whereby those societies which are appropriate environments for human development can be distinguished from those which are not.

The first way of tackling this question might be to deny

that human nature and human development have a social content, and so an individual is able to maximize his powers and actualize his potentialities even in a hostile environment. This answer might meet the problem by making the form of society irrelevant. But this solution will hardly do for the caseworker because he is clearly concerned with the relationship between self-development and the environment. Apart from this specific difficulty it is doubtful whether a very strong 'inner redoubt' theory of the self can be maintained. It might be argued that only peripheral human capacities remain relatively untouched by society. All the central human powers are structured by, and given content by, society. Men's potentialities are not just given, they are given by the social context, by the standards of the community in which the person lives, moves and has his being. Indeed it might be that this is more true today than at any time in history, in view of the nature and scope of advertising and the pervasive nature of the communications industry in our society. MacIntyre has drawn attention to this point (1968, p. 7):

> Nobody knows better than those who control advertising, television and social surveys that desires and tastes are not simple, given, indubitable entities. They have to be and always can be solicited. They do not exist in a vacuum waiting for an object. What we desire depends entirely upon what objects of desire have been and are presented to us. We learn to want things. Our desires have a history, and not just a biological natural history, but a rational history of intelligible response to what we are offered.

The same is true of other human functions and capacities. Human beings respond to the images and paradigms of human nature which are presented in society. There can be no headlong retreat into the 'inner citadel' or the 'inner redoubt'. Human possibilities are social and are determined by something prominent in the social structure, whether it be the mode of production, a set of metaphysical beliefs or the ethos of a particular social class. The optimal development of a person's individuality and the realization of his potentialities cannot be achieved except within society. It is only if the images and paradigms of human thought and action are changed in a particular society—a society which is not conducive to human development, which is not a community—that the society can be changed. This, of course, presents a difficult problem. How can this change be wrought? Individuals cannot change themselves, because the content of their individuality is given by society, yet how can society change if individuals cannot? Marcuse makes the following point against the possibility of an individualistic solution to this problem (he is referring to Erich Fromm whom Marcuse accused of taking the individualistic solution) (1968, p. 203):

> He speaks of the productive realization of the personality, of care, responsibility, and a respect for one's fellow men, of productive love and happiness—as if a man could actually practice all this and remain sane and full of well being in a society which Fromm himself describes as one of total alienation, dominated by the commodity relationships of the market.

An individualistic solution to the problem of mental health and community cannot be provided, yet surely this problem needs to be solved. Images are plentiful, but blueprints which are conceptually coherent and practically possible are not in such generous supply. Of course, casework theorists are aware of these problems, but in the works of both theorists and critics problems are stated, solutions are not offered. Among critics Wootton (1967, p. 218) is an advocate of reform rather than therapy to help people to come to terms with '. . . totalitarian methods of government, the dingy culture of an urban slum, the contemporary English law of marriage, or what I have elsewhere called the standards of an acquisitive, competitive, hierarchical, envious society'. This is in fact a denial of the humane concern of caseworkers. As a caseworker says (Lurie, Kasius 1954, p. 50): 'Social work will lose much of its meaning if social workers do not remain alert to the implications of unsatisfactory mores and social institutions in their own lives and the lives of others.'

The difficulty is to conceptualize this concern. Adjustment to a society is only a meaningful way in which human personalities can be developed if that society can fully mobilize the capacities of its members, if there seems to be no meaningful distinction to be drawn between the standards of a society and the deepest springs of human thought and action. Before models of casework activity conceived in these terms are offered in the next chapter possibly it is appropriate to close this one with an image of such a close relationship between the individual and his social activities. The image of the dancer and the dance is from Yeats's poem, 'Among School Children', which is quoted by MacIntyre (1968):

> Labour is blossoming or dancing where
> The body is not bruised to pleasure soul,
> Nor beauty born out of its own despair,
> Nor bleary-eyed wisdom out of midnight oil.
> O Chestnut tree, great-rooted blossomer,
> Are you the leaf, the blossom or the bole?
> O body swayed to music, O brightening glance,
> How can we know the dancer from the dance?

4

Therapy, reform, or revolution:
an insoluble conflict?

What are the roots that clutch, what branches grow
Out of this stony rubbish? Son of man,
You cannot say, or guess, for you know only
A heap of broken images, where the sun beats,
And the dead tree gives no shelter, the cricket no relief,
And the dry stone no sound of water.

(T. S. Eliot: 'The Waste Land')

The basic conflict in the previous chapter arose over the
function of the caseworker. Should the caseworker provide therapy, that is to say, help people to come to terms
with the reality of their social situation? Or is the essential
casework function that of reform or revolution, that is to
say, radically changing the structure of society so that it
can be experienced as a community? That this conflict is
central not only for casework, but for our culture
generally, can be seen from the following perceptive comment by Bantock (1960, p. 71):

Behind this conflict over reform or therapy, of which
Barbara Wootton's book is only one example, we note,
it seems to me, a fundamental cleavage of opinion in
the modern world arising out of two quite distinct
assessments of human nature. Behind the concern for
therapy lies Freud's sombre theory of the human situation, one involving the conflict between individual,
instinctual biological urges, and the demands of social
life. The pleasure principle and the reality principle are,
even at best, in an uneasy relationship, necessitating on
the part of the individual, repression and sublimation,
and resting on the precarious strength of the ego structure. . . . The other view is more optimistic in outlook.
It tends to dissolve human personality into a set of

74

potential social attributes, and thus never loses sight of the possibility that social changes may be brought about which will reflect men's needs more fully, or that harmonious adjustment between individual desire and social reality may be possible.

This latter theory which Bantock discusses seems to involve considerable logical difficulties. If the human personality is dissolved into a set of social attributes, then it seems difficult to see how one could ever accommodate social change. One cannot change individuals without changing society, because the personalities of men are social products; on the other hand it seems difficult to see how one can change a society without changing individuals. The theory is inadequate at a conceptual level; change waits upon both individuals and society, and yet both stand at the open door of change like two eighteenth-century French courtiers not wishing to commit the solecism of going through the door first.

Does this imply that therapy is inevitable? If Bantock's second possibility proves to be an illusion, does this imply a commitment to Freudianism and the conservatism and pessimism about the possibilities of social improvement which seem to be implied by this theory? It might be argued that, so far as casework is concerned, a commitment to a Freudian view is presupposed, but on the other hand this does not entail that such a view is necessarily socially conservative.

It seems to be an implication of Freud's theory in *Civilisation and Its Discontents* (1963) that there can be no society which does justice to men's powers and capacities. Life in society is a matter of more or less adjustment, but there is no perfect relationship between man and society to be obtained. Man cannot have the authentic experience of being a member of a community —consequently the emphasis in psychoanalysis on therapy;

and the same emphasis is to be found in casework. There can be no ideal solution to the problem of social life, so casework should help people to come to terms with the reality of their social situation. All societies involve a repression of human capacities and powers, and consequently maladjustment is endemic in *all* societies.

The tragic nature of social life: the work of Freud

In Freud's view there can be no civilization, no society, no culture which can fully express man's nature and truly fulfil men's capacities and powers, because the very existence of society depends upon the sublimation of certain instincts, and even the repression of those instincts. Men, in Freud's view, are radically amphibious. They live in two dimensions: the realm of instinctual drives dominated by the pleasure principle, and social existence controlled and directed in the individual case by the reality principle. Man under the rule of the pleasure principle is a creature of animal drives, particularly concerned with sexual gratification, seeking to maximize his own pleasure and avoid painful experiences. These drives, Freud argues (1963): '. . . strive for nothing but for gaining pleasure; from any operation which might arouse unpleasantness, mental activity draws back.' But as Hobbes noticed before Freud, this seeking after pleasure and gratification is incompatible with the existence of society. In social life the full and painless gratification of human desires is impossible, because it brings the individual into contact with other like-minded individuals. The realization of this, which in the individual case happens in early childhood, leads to a modification of the principle and the domination of the reality principle. This is embodied in the institutions, mores and standards within which a child is reared and which parents, teachers and caseworkers help him to accept. The ascendancy of the reality principle over the pleasure principle alters the conception of pleasure. Instinctual pleasures and drives are sublimated into socially accepted practices or are repressed in the name of the reality principle (1963, p. 34):

> . . . instincts are induced to displace the conditions of their satisfaction, to lead into other paths. In most cases this coincides with that of sublimation of instinctual aims with which we are familiar. . . . Sublimation of instinct is an especially conspicuous feature of cultural development; it is what makes it possible for the higher psychical activities, scientific, artistic, or ideological, to play such an important part in civilised life. . . . Finally, and this seems most important of all, it is impossible to overlook the extent to which civilization is built upon the renunciation of instincts, how much it presupposes precisely the non-satisfaction (by suppression, repression or other means) of powerful instincts. This cultural frustration dominates a large field of the social relationships between human beings.

Civilization has a value because the 'higher psychical activities' play a large and valuable role in human life, but these activities depend for their existence upon the sublimation or repression of much more powerful instincts of human beings. The kind of sublimation which Freud has in mind here is, for example, the sublimation of anal erotic desires into a group of socially acceptable, and even socially desirable character traits such as parsimony, a passion for order and cleanliness (see Freud 1963, p. 33). In place of the insecure, temporary and destructive pleasures to be gained from adherence to the pleasure principle, following the constraints of the reality principle brings a more certain gratification of socially accepted pleasures, or for the sublimation of unacceptable pleasures. This gratification is more restrained; it may not be so immediate, but it is more or less guaranteed. Clearly, however, obedience to the dictates of the reality principle involves more than a modification of man's instinctual life, it rather involves a fundamental change in it. Marcuse makes this point very forcibly (1969, p. 30):

> However, the psychoanalytic interpretation reveals that the reality principle enforces a change not only in the form and timing of the pleasure, but in its very substance. The adjustment of pleasure to the reality principle implies the subjugation and diversion of the destructive forces of instinctual gratification, of its incompatibility with the established societal norms and relations, and by that token implies the transubstantiation of pleasure itself.

Freud argues that this repression and sublimation in the name of the reality principle, which is the very condition of social life, produces neurosis. He argues, for example, that the sexual life of man in a civilized community is severely impaired. Only heterosexual genital love has been saved from repression because such a mode of sexuality is itself a necessary condition of the continuance of the civilization (1963, p. 42):

> Present-day civilization makes it plain that it will only permit sexual relations on the basis of an indissoluble bond between one man and one woman, and it does not like sexuality as a source of pleasure in its own right, and is only prepared to tolerate it because there is so far no substitute for it as a means of propagating the human race.

It is this restriction of sexual activity which causes neurosis, creating a tension between inner drives and social requirements, which leads to problems in the individual's social functioning. This restriction of basic drives according to the requirements of the reality principle is, in Freud's

78

view, endemic in any sort of society. There is always a tension between the one and the many, between man and society. It follows that only by some kind of self-deception can a man experience his society as a community, because being a member of a community involves, as we have seen a deep identity between the deepest springs of human action, and the standards and norms of the community, an identity which Freud seems to imply can never hold.

Given the fact of the great influence of Freud on casework theory, it is probable that this part of his theory has deeply influenced the approach of casework theorists to the problems of the relationship between man and society. The need on the Freudian view is for therapy, to help people to come to terms with their social reality, not so much for reform because problems of social functioning are endemic in any society whatever. There can be no ideal community to which all will feel deeply attached, which fully expresses and satisfies the ideals, desires and instincts of the individuals who live in that society. The problem is to help those who are particularly maladjusted to the claims of society to come to terms with them. Casework can, therefore, use Freud's views here as a defence of what might be called the realism of the casework profession in the face of the existence of social morality. Submission to the reality principle, or to the claims of social morality, is a central feature of civilized human life in society. Casework is an attempt to deal in a humanistic way with the problems thrown up by the tension between the pleasure principle and the reality principle. This is a point which Bantock makes (1960, p. 72):

> The concern with therapy then depends upon the notion of a basic personality structure, impaired through early family experiences, which can be brought back into

some sort of essentially and necessarily restricted harmony with social demands.

The possibility of reform or revolution as a casework aim presupposes the view that some societies are less repressive than others, that some societies may be better objects of human adjustment, and constitute environments which can enable man to live both in harmony with it and his own inner drives and motivations. This possibility is apparently denied by the Freudian theory; Freudianism and the corresponding model of casework as therapy seems to be intractably pessimistic and conservative. Some theorists have argued, on the contrary, that Freud's theory can be used for reformist, or even revolutionary ends and if this is so then the same possibilities would be opened up for casework. It is emphasized at this point in the discussion that in analysing these three models of casework—therapy, reform, or revolution—the author is not to be taken as recommending one rather than the other. Rather the aim is to uncover the assumptions and implications of each view so that those whose practice involves problems of this sort may have a clearer view of the issues.

The possibility of reform in the interests of mental health

Among the most eminent of those who use Freudian psychoanalytical theory for the purpose of advocating reforms in the interests of mental health by changing contemporary atomistic societies into truly human communities, is Eric Fromm in his work *The Sane Society* (1963). Fromm rejects the rather pessimistic, quietist approach to social experience which is implicit in the work of Freud. He argues rather, that society can be changed in the interests of human development and the realization of all men's capacities. He points out quite correctly that social life for man is, in Freud's view, a tragedy (1963, p. 76):

> Primitive man is healthy and happy because he is not
> frustrated in his basic instincts, but he lacks the blessings
> of culture. Civilized man is more secure, enjoys art and
> science, but he is bound to be neurotic because of the
> continued frustrations of his instincts unreformed by
> civilization.

Fromm argues that this theory as it stands, is a distortion.
Society is doubtless in conflict with the asocial aspects of
man's being, in particular his demand for sexual gratification, but it can also be in conflict with man's most
valuable human qualities which certain societies may
repress and distort. Societies can be judged in terms of
the harm and distortion which they inflict on these qualities. Fromm appears to reject the view that the content
of human nature, the images and paradigms of human
thought and action, are *totally* given and structured by
society. If so, then human nature can be used as a critical
tool or standard by which a society can be assessed. These
essential, but not socially-given human attributes are, for
example, a desire for happiness, harmony, love and freedom; these are inherent in the very nature of man. Some
societies provide the appropriate forms of social experience
for the achievement and the satisfaction of these desires;
others do not, but either distort or do not attempt to
satisfy these basic longings. Social problems are endemic
only in these societies. Contemporary capitalist societies
belong to this latter category. They do not provide a
community in which men can act out their deepest desires
and instincts. Fromm argues that in such societies man is
alienated (1963, p. 120):

> By alienation is meant a mode of experiences in which
> a person experiences himself as an alien. He has become,
> one might say, estranged from the world. He does not

experience himself as the centre of his world, as the creator of his own acts, but his acts and their consequences have become his masters whom he obeys, or whom he may even worship.

Alienation is, in Fromm's view, a form of mental ill health. The neurotic personality is an alienated personality, in that the person is a stranger to his own actions. Capitalism as a form of social organization does not merely suppress or cause the sublimation of the pleasure principle instincts —a feature of any society; rather it goes much further in that it distorts certain central human capacities.

In order to change society in the interests of mental health, to maximize the achievement of harmony, love and freedom, and to minimize alienation and estrangement, Fromm advocates certain reforms. In a chapter called 'Roads to Sanity' he puts forward fairly detailed proposals. While Fromm seeks to bring Freudian and socialist insights together, he argues that a purely economic change in the infrastructure of capitalism will not suffice. He argues (1963, p. 271) that sanity and mental health:

> ... can be attained only by simultaneous changes in the sphere of industrial and political organization, of spiritual and philosophical orientations, of character structure and of cultural activities. The concentration of effort in any one of these spheres to the exclusion of others is destructive of all change.

Fromm argues that these changes are within the social democratic tradition, and in formulating his proposals, he often refers to the work of Crosland, Crossman and Jenkins in *New Fabian Essays* (1951). He advocates control by the people of the commanding heights of the economy, worker participation in industrial decision making in order to rehumanize work, political decentralization, a reformation of education so that educational processes can generate the spiritual renewal required, and a rediscovery of ritual and corporate arts in order that men may come together again as human beings. Fromm's aim is clearly to advocate a communitarian society, one in which people can feel at home because they are closely involved with one another at all levels. Again it is interesting to see that Fromm argues what is in fact a moral thesis in terms of what appears to be the scientific concept of mental health. Common forms of experience are vitally necessary for the development of community (1963, p. 349):

> The transformation of an atomistic into a communitarian society depends upon creating again the opportunity for people to sing together, dance together, and admire together—together and not as members of a lonely crowd.

Fromm visualizes his new community in the following way (1963, p. 276):

> What society corresponds to this aim of mental health, and what would be the structure of the sane society? First of all a society in which no man is a means to another's end, but always without exception an end in himself; hence where nobody is used, nor uses himself for purposes which are not those of the unfolding of his human powers; where man is at the centre, and where all economic and political activities are subordinated to the aim of his growth. A sane society is one in which qualities like greed, exploitativeness, possessiveness, narcissism, have no chance to be used for greater material gain, or for the enhancement of one's own personal prestige. Where acting in accordance with one's conscience is looked upon as a fundamental and necessary quality, and where opportunism and lack of principles is deemed to be asocial; where the individual is concerned with social matters so that they become

83

personal matters; where his relationships with his fellow men are not separated from his relationships in the private sphere. A sane society furthermore is one which puts a man to operate within manageable and observable dimensions and to be an active participant in the life of society as well as in his own life. It is one which furthers human solidarity and not only permits but stipulates its members to relate themselves to each other lovingly; a sane society furthers the productive activity of everybody in his work, stimulates the unfolding of reason and induces men to give expression to inner needs in collective art and rituals.

Two points might be made here: in the first place it is clear how Fromm's idea of the 'sane' society is closely related to Williams's idea of the community of which people can feel that they are members because they find the ways of life in their community deeply expressive of their needs and aspirations; the second point is to recall the comment by Thomas Szasz—'Mental Health and illness are new ways of describing moral values'. Fromm's thesis is given a certain amount of cogency because he links the idea of community, which is a moral notion, so closely with that of sanity, which seems to be a scientific one.

Fromm sees some prospect of social reform in the interests of mental health, a prospect which did not seem to be a part of Freud's own theory. It seems that Fromm is still willing to allow that any society must repress certain sexual instincts, but he argues that contemporary capitalist societies distort and repress other basic desires, for example the desire for freedom, for love and for harmony. Whereas capitalist societies are atomistic, and constitute a society of strangers, the sane society will be a community with which people are deeply involved.

The feasibility of Fromm's proposals depends, of course, upon his being able to formulate a view of human capacities and potentialities which are not dependent upon society, since only then can he use such a conception as a critical tool in terms of which he can assess the repressiveness of a particular society. Only if one already has conception of what is essential to man can one use this conception to show that these essential attributes are denied realization in a particular society. If, on the other hand, the content of human nature is given by a society, it is difficult to see how this could then be a critical tool in the analysis of society. Fromm clearly thinks that it is possible to formulate a conception of human nature which will give some orientation to programmes for social reform. This possibility is partly denied by Herbert Marcuse. In *Eros and Civilisation* (1969) Marcuse argues that there is no reformist middle way between therapy and revolution. Either the content of human nature, and the paradigms of thought and action are socially given or they have some completely transcending content; in which case to operate within the given paradigms and to seek to modify them in terms of the transcending ones is impossible. Either a man has to be helped to come to terms with what are considered to be socially accepted standards of conduct as they in fact exist, or these standards have to be done away with because they are inimical to the development of man's ideal personality, the conception of man's attributes and powers which is the negation of the one presupposed in society (1969, p. 203):

> *Either* one defines personality and individuality in terms of their possibilities within the established form of civilization, in which case then realization is for the majority tantamount to successful adjustment. *Or* one defines them in terms of their transcending content, including their socially denied possibilities beyond and beneath their actual existence; in this case self-realization would imply transgression beyond the established forms of civilization, to radically new modes of per-

sonality and individuality incompatible with the prevailing ones. Today this would mean curing the patient to become a rebel, or (which is saying the same thing) a martyr.

The dilemma here for casework is clear. If one of the central aims of casework is to facilitate the realization on the part of the individual of his powers, capacities and capabilities, then is he to help the individual to come to terms with the socially accepted standards of self-realization? But what if these can be regarded as in some sense distortions of human potentialities? Is one of the casework functions to promote reform in society in order to facilitate the emergence of new standards of personality? If so, is this aim at all feasible? And how could the social worker who is often regarded as in some sense the agent of society justify such a political commitment? Or is the only way to seek a revolution? If the patterns of human activity and the claims of society upon individuals are so distorted, is it possible to modify them from within? In such a society, it might be argued, those who are classified as social deviants could be regarded as gesturing towards a better (more sane) social order. The work of Marcuse is interesting at this point because he takes up this revolutionary position on the basis of an acceptance and extension of Freudian theory, which as we have seen, appears to be intractably conservative and pessimistic about the possibility of social change in the interests of human development.

Eros and Civilization: *the possibility of revolution*

Marcuse argues that although the Freudian theory does appear to be conservative and pessimistic at a superficial level, it does contain within itself the seeds of a critical theory of society. He agrees with Freud that a certain level of repression appears to be necessary for the existence of civilization and culture, but he argues that the amount of repression present in contemporary Western societies cannot be justified or explained in terms of necessary conditions for the preservation of society. In order to facilitate the analysis of this fact Marcuse seeks to refine the concept of repression which is so central to Freudian theory. He argues that two sorts of repression can be distinguished: *basic repression* and *surplus repression*. Basic repression is the form of repression which it seems has to exist in order for there to be civilization at all; some modification and restriction of instinctual gratification is necessary for the existence of society. Contemporary society, however, involves far more repression than is necessary to secure its existence; this is surplus repression. Surplus repression is needed not so much to secure the existence of civilized life as such, but rather a particular form of social organization, a society with a particular ethos and culture. In Marcuse's view the kind of society which surplus repression is used to maintain is a society based upon class domination. Surplus repression will disappear when class domination and the capitalist system which underpins it is abolished. Therapists who seek to help people to come to terms with the existing patterns of behaviour and the existing claims of society upon the individual are in fact helping people to come to terms with a repressive society, with a civilization which cannot do justice to the possibilities of human nature (1968, p. 251):

Is not the individual who functions normally, adequately, and healthily as a citizen of a sick society—is not such an individual himself sick? And would not a sick society require an antagonistic concept of mental health, a meta-concept designating (and preserving) mental qualities which are tabooed, arrested or distorted by the 'sanity' prevalent in the sick society? (For example, mental health equals the ability to live as a dissenter, to live a non-adjusted life.)

As a tentative definition of 'sick society' we can say that a society is sick when its basic institutions . . . do not permit the use of the available material and intellectual resources for the optimal development and satisfaction of individual needs. The larger the discrepancy between the potential and actual human conditions, the greater the social need for what I term 'surplus repression', that is, repression necessitated not by the growth and preservation of society but by vested interests in maintaining an established society. Such surplus repression introduces . . . new strains and stresses in the individual.

In a society in which there is no surplus repression, Marcuse argues that even basic repression will become unnecessary. Without the distortions imposed upon human nature by the surplus repression of a sick society, basic human needs and drives will be transformed and instead of being egotistical and asocial will become co-operative and creative. Consequently, a society without repression is possible, a society which will fully satisfy all human needs. Such a society cannot be achieved without a revolution. Marcuse contemplates the possibility of revolution in contemporary capitalist societies in *One Dimensional Man* (1964), and he argues that revolution is only possible in so far as there is some 'negative' element in society which stands in contradiction to the generally accepted beliefs and standards of that society. Marx and other socialist revolutionaries always considered that this negative element would comprise the proletariat along with certain intellectual sympathizers. Marcuse rejects this possibility—the proletariat has become reconciled to welfare capitalism, it is much a part of the *status quo* as any other social group. The negative element in Marcuse's view will consist of all those

who, for one reason and another, find themselves maladjusted to the distorted standards of society. Many of the
people who come to caseworkers would constitute a
potential membership for this negative element in society.

In helping people to adjust to the established state of
society, casework is counter-revolutionary; it is involved
in arresting the development of a revolutionary consciousness on the part of those who are maladjusted to the claims
of a sick society. In Marcuse's view, in order to achieve the
casework aim of satisfactory human development, caseworkers should become revolutionaries.

Casework: its moral, social, and political engagement

In this chapter three possible models of casework practice
have been considered. One, which might be called the
realist therapeutic approach, is based upon a humani-
tarian concern to help people who have problems in their
social functioning, and scepticism about the possibility
of achieving a society in which human adjustment will be
no longer a problem because the society does full justice
to human needs, drives and instincts. The second and third
possibilities, the reformist and revolutionary approaches,
agree in seeing the structure of society at fault. Human
beings have problems in their social functioning because
the society in which they are to function cannot do justice
to people's most intimate needs. These two approaches
differ, however, in their assessment of the ways in which a
society adequate to human life can be achieved. These two
approaches also involve major difficulties for casework, in
that a great deal of casework is done in the name of the
claims which existing society has to make on individuals.
Most casework theorists emphasize that they do share a
dual concern, not only with the individual, but also with
society: they are in some sense, as Miles (1954) says,

representatives of society.

These are models and possibilities; it is not for the philosopher *qua* philosopher to recommend one or the other, rather to try to understand the presuppositions and implications of theories, in this case with reference to casework. What is clear, however, is that implicitly at least the theory and practice of social casework raise in an immediate and important manner some of the most difficult problems of social and political theory. Halmos may be correct when he argues in *The Faith of the Counsellors* (1965) that the motivation to the counselling professions, and to casework in particular, may be a distrust of politics and political solutions, but I hope that this book has shown that someone who does enter the profession with this motivation is in fact making a decision based upon a false asssessment of what is involved in the practice of casework. If the arguments of this book are correct, then it could be argued that the caseworker is more involved with social and political commitments of one form or another than the average citizen or the average worker.

Suggestions for further reading

In order to tie these suggestions closely with the points made in the text, the list of recommended books is divided into the same sub-sections as the book.

Chapter 1: Introductory and programmatic

Unfortunately, in view of its unquestioned importance, the theory and practice of social casework has received very little attention from professional philosophers, and it is to be hoped that in the future a comparable amount of time and effort will be spent on the analysis of casework concepts by the philosopher as is now spent on the philosophy of education. In view of this lack of interest, there are no general books which deal specifically with casework. *Freedom and Community* by N. HAINES (1966) deals with some of the problems encountered in this work and the book is useful in that it is directed towards people who are engaged in serving the community in some manner, but again it does not deal specifically with casework concepts. Similar problems to those encountered in casework theory are also to be found in the theory of education, and the reader could profitably look at R. S. PETERS, *Ethics and*

Education (1966). Peters is also the part-author of a general work on moral and social philosophy which contains many discussions of interest to caseworkers, R. S. PETERS, and S. I. BENN, *Social Principles and the Democratic State* (1959).

There is no readily intelligible book which would act as a suitable introduction to the current mode of philosophizing in Britain and the United States of America. The work of leading figures such as Austin, Wittgenstein, Strawson and Ayer, is generally far too technical and divorced from casework concerns to act as introductory material. One book which does give the background to contemporary Anglo-Saxon philosophy is A. J. AYER (ed.), *The Revolution in Philosophy* (1957). However, caseworkers who are interested in pursuing some of the intricacies of modern philosophy may find it more congenial to approach the subject through moral philosophy. Central books in this field are: S. TOULMIN, *The Place of Reason in Ethics* (1950); P. NOWELL-SMITH, *Ethics* (1954); R. M. HARE, *The Language of Morals* and *Freedom and Reason* (1952 and 1963, respectively). The best recent work on social and political philosophy is to be found in the series, *Philosophy, Politics and Society I, II, III*, edited by P. LASLETT, and W. G. RUNCIMAN (1956, 1962 and 1967, respectively).

Chapter 2: Social and moral theory in casework

A good general work which deals with many of the problems raised in this chapter is D. EMMET, *Rules, Roles and Relations* (1966). In this work Professor Emmet discusses the inadequacies of a purely personalist concept of morality, based upon subjective decision-making, as in the work of Hare (see above) and she tries to bring a philosophical understanding of morality into line with sociological insights into role behaviour. The concept of respect for persons is discussed by B. WILLIAMS in an article on 'Equality' in P. LASLETT and W. G. RUNCIMAN, *Philosophy, Politics and Society, Series II* (see above); by R. S. PETERS and S. I. BENN, *Social Principles and the Democratic State* (see above); and in R. S. PETERS, *Ethics and Education* (see above).

There are, of course, any number of books on existentialism, but still the best is Sartre's own introductory lecture, J. P. SARTRE, *Existentialism is Humanism* (1948). This short introductory work contains all those elements of existentialism which are of professional interest to the caseworker: the critiques of role acceptance and social morality and the concept of bad faith. The opposite kind of perspective is to be gained from the work of E. GOFFMAN which is cited in the Bibliography. Also of interest here as a foil to Sartre's views are such works by E. DURKHEIM as *The Division of Labour in Society* (1966) and *Suicide* (1966).

Chapter 3: Community and mental health

Books on this topic vary tremendously in the extremity of the case which they argue. Among the most extreme is R. D. LAING, *The Politics of Experience and the Bird of Paradise* (1967). Less extreme but still highly critical of the concept of mental health is T. SZASZ, 'The Mental Health Ethic', in R. T. DE GEORGE (ed.): *Ethics and Society* (1968). B. WOOTTON is another vigorous critic in her *Social Science and Social Pathology* (1967). An interesting article which has things of importance to say for casework is R. S. PETERS, 'Mental Health as an Educational Aim', in T. B. HOLLINS (ed.), *Aims in Education* (1968). MICHEL FOUCAULT provides an historical perspective to the concept in his *Madness and Civilisation* (1967).

Chapter 4: Therapy, reform or revolution?

A good general introduction to the work of Freud is P. RIEFF, *Freud: The Mind of a Moralist* (1960). A. MACINTYRE provides a vigorous critique of contemporary society from a non-sectarian point of view in his 'Against Utilitarianism', in T. B. HOLLINS (ed.): *Aims in Education* (see above). Ideas of H. MARCUSE which may interest caseworkers are to be found in his collection of essays, *Negations* (1968); M. CRANSTON has provided an exposition and critique of his work in 'Herbert Marcuse', in *Encounter*, March 1969.

Bibliography

APTEKAR, H. H. (1955) *The Dynamics of Casework Counselling*, New York: Houghton Mifflin.

BACHRACH, P. (1967) *The Theory of Democratic Elitisim: a Critique*, Boston and Toronto: Little, Brown.

BANTOCK, G. H. (1960) 'A Comment on "Reform and Therapy",' in 'Moral Issues in the Training of Social Workers', *The Sociological Review Monograph No. 3*, The University of Keele Press.

BENN, S. I. and PETERS, R. S. (1959) *Social Principles and the Democratic State*, George Allen & Unwin.

BERLIN, I. (1958) *Two Concepts of Liberty*, The Clarendon Press.

BIESTEK, F. (1961) *The Casework Relationship*, Allen & Unwin.

BOTTOMORE, T. B. (1966) *Elites and Society*, Penguin.

BOWLBY, J. (1952) *Maternal Care and Mental Health*, World Health Organisation.

BRADLEY, F. H. (1962) *Ethical Studies*, The Clarendon Press.

CORGIAT, R. (1954) Art. in *New Trends of European Social Work*, Vienna: Astrorvadruck.

CRICK, B. (1964) *In Defence of Politics*, Penguin Books.

DAHRENDORF, R. (1968) *Essays in the Theory of Society*, Routledge & Kegan Paul.

BIBLIOGRAPHY

DAVIS, K. (1938) 'Mental Hygiene and Class Structure', *Psychiatry*, February, 1938.

DONNISON, D. (1955) 'Observations on University Training for Social Work in Great Britain and North America', *Social Service Review*, December 1955.

DURKHEIM, E. (1953) *Sociology and Philosophy*, Cohen & West.

EATON, J. W. (1951) 'The Assessment of Mental Health', *American Journal of Psychiatry*, August 1951.

EMMET, D. (1966) *Rules, Roles and Relations*, Macmillan.

FORTUNE, R. (1932) *Sorcerers of Dobu*, Routledge & Kegan Paul.

FREUD, S. (1963) *Civilisation and its Discontents*, Hogarth Press. (1914) *Psychopathology for Everyday Life*, Benn.

FROMM, E. (1963) *The Sane Society*, Routledge & Kegan Paul.

GELLNER, E. (1966) *Thought and Change*, Weidenfeld & Nicholson.

GOFFMAN, E. (1968) *Where the Action Is*, Penguin.

GOFFMAN, E. (1968) *The Presentation of Self in Everyday Life*, Penguin.

HALMOS, P. (1965) *The Faith of the Counsellors*, Constable.

HAMILTON, G. (1950) 'The Underlying Philosophy of Social Casework', *Principles and Techniques in Social Casework*, ed. C. Kasius, New York: Family Service Association of America.

HARRIS, E. E. (1968) 'Respect for Persons', *Ethics and Society*, ed. R. T. De George, Macmillan.

HOLLIS, F. (1940) *Social Casework in Practice*, New York: Family Service Association of America.

HUME, D. (1964) *A Treatise of Human Nature*, ed. Selby-Bigge, The Clarendon Press.

HUTCHINSON, D. (1946) 'A Re-examination of Some Aspects of Casework Practice in Adoption', *Child Welfare League of America*, Bulletin No. 25, November 1946.

KARIEL, H. S. (1961) *The Decline of American Pluralism*, Stanford: The University Press.

KASIUS, C. (1950) *Principles and Techniques in Social Casework*, New York: Family Service Association of America. (1954) *New Directions in Social Work*, New York: Harper.

LAING, R. D. (1967) *The Politics of Experience and the Bird of Paradise*, Penguin.

LANE, L. C. (1952) 'The Aggressive to Preventive Casework with Children's Problems', *Social Casework*, Vol. 33. February 1952

LURIE, H. L. (1954) 'The Responsibilities of a Socially Oriented Profession', in *New Directions in Social Work*, ed. C. Kasius.

MACINTYRE, A. (1968) 'Against Utilitarianism', *Aims in Education*, ed. T. B. Hollins, Manchester University Press.

MACPHERSON, C. B. (1965) *The Real World of Democracy*, Toronto: The Canadian Broadcasting Corporation.

MARCUSE, H. (1964) *One Dimensional Man*, Routledge & Kegan Paul. (1968) *Negations*, Penguin. (1969) *Eros and Civilisation*, Sphere Books.

MARX, K. (1844) *Economic and Philosophical Manuscripts of 1844*, New York: International Publishers 1964.

MILES, A. P. (1954) *American Social Work Theory*, New York: Harper & Row.

MILL, J. S. (1920) *Essay on Liberty*, Dent, Everyman Edition.

MOFFETT, J. (1968) *Concepts in Casework Treatment*, Routledge & Kegan Paul.

PARRY, G. B. (1969) *Political Elites*, Allen & Unwin.

PERLMAN, H. H. (1953) 'Social Components of Social Casework Practice', *Social Welfare Forum* 1953. (1951) 'The Caseworker's Use of Collateral Information, *Social Casework*, Vol. 32, No. 8. 1951. (1957) *Social Casework, A Problem Solving Process*, Chicago: The University Press.

PETERS, R. S. (1960) *The Concept of Motivation*, Routledge & Kegan Paul. (1968) 'Mental Health as an Educational

Aim', *Aims in Education*, ed. T. B. Hollins, Manchester University Press.

PETERS, R. S. and BENN, S. I. (1959) *Social Principles and the Democratic State*, Allen & Unwin.

POLLARD, B. (1962) *Social Casework for the State*, Pall Mall Press.

RICHMOND, M. (1930) *The Long View*, New York: The Russell Sage Foundation.

ROBINSON, V. (1930) *A Changing Psychology in Social Casework*, Chapel Hill, Philadelphia: University of North Carolina.

ROUSSEAU, E. (1947) *The Social Contract*, Dent, Everyman Edition.

SARTRE, J. P. (1955) 'Materialism and Revolution', *Literary and Philosophical Essays*, Rider Co.

SODDY, K. (1962) *Cross Cultural Studies in Mental Health, Mental Health and Value Systems*, Tavistock Publications.

SZASZ, T. (1968) 'The Mental Health Ethic', in *Ethics and Society*, ed. R. T. De George, Macmillan.

THIBAUT, W. (1943) 'The Concept of Normality in Clinical Psychology', *Psychological Review*, May 1963.

TIMMS, N. (1964) *Social Casework*, Routledge & Kegan Paul. (1968) *The Language of Social Casework*, Routledge & Kegan Paul.

TOWLE, C. (1954) *The Learner in Education for the Professions*, Chicago: The University Press.

UNITED NATIONS ORGANISATION (1955) *The Prevention of Juvenile Delinquency in Selected Countries*, New York: U. N. Publications.

WILLIAMS, R. (1965) *The Long Revolution*, Penguin.

WILSON, J. (1965) *Logic and Sexual Morality*, Penguin Books.

WOOTTON, B. (1967) *Social Science and Social Pathology*, Allen & Unwin.

WORLD HEALTH ORGANISATION (1951) *Expert Committee on Mental Health, Report of the Second Session*, Geneva: W.H.O. Publications.

YOUNGHUSBAND, E. (1967) *Social Work and Social Values*, Allen & Unwin.

DATE DUE

APR 30 '81	APR 23 '81		

DEMCO 38-297